Snow Blind

Snow Blind

Douglas Kalajian

RavensYard Publishing, Ltd.
Fairfax County, Virginia

© 2000 Douglas Kalajian

All Rights Reserved
Manufactured in the United States of America

ISBN 0-9667883-8-9

Library of Congress Catalogue Card Number: 00-100882

No part of this book may be reproduced or transmitted by any
means, electronic or mechanical, except by written permission from
RavensYard Publishing, Ltd. except for inclusion in a review.

Published by
RavensYard Publishing, Ltd.
P.O. Box 176
Oakton, Virginia 22124
USA
www.ravensyard.com

*This book is dedicated to
Robyn and Mandy Kalajian*

Howard's path

Preface 9

Introduction 11

The People close to Howard 14

Chapter One — Two men on trial, *looking back to the beginning 17*

Chapter Two — In the belly of the '60s, *the origin of Howard's ideals 26*

Chapter Three — Zen in the '70s, *a time when nothing could go wrong 38*

Chapter Four — The eyes of truth, *when Howard turns away and gets lost 51*

Chapter Five — Into the '80s, alone, *as Howard turns inward from fear 62*

Chapter Six — A leader lost, *the danger of being a follower 75*

Chapter Seven — Fire in the night, *the violence all around closes in 79*

Chapter Eight — Settling accounts, *a close call with the mob 88*

Chapter Nine — Losing his balance, *the addiction becomes harder to hide 92*

Chapter Ten — Sharing the blame, *Donna is drawn into his sickness 102*

Chapter Eleven	First poison, then suicide, *Donna's hope evaporates* *108*
Chapter Twelve	Killing Howard, *Donna strikes back* *118*
Chapter Thirteen:	A jury that won't listen, *friends insist Howard face the truth* *126*
Chapter Fourteen	Learning to live, *Howard finally gives up* *133*
Chapter Fifteen	One last lesson, *Howard gets the advice he needs* *139*
Chapter Sixteen	The verdict, *Howard passes a crucial test* *147*
Chapter Seventeen	A gladiator once more, *Howard wins again in court* *156*
Chapter Eighteen	Making Sense in the '90s, *Howard learns to live with the past* *164*
Chapter Nineteen	Only human, *Howard accepts his limits* *168*
Chapter Twenty	Two familiar voices, *Howard begins to earn his second chance* *173*
	Redemption: An epilogue *176*
	Other ends *179*
	About the author *180*

Preface

Howard Finkelstein made this work possible by sharing his memories, files and scrapbooks, and he and Donna both shared their deepest feelings. Howard also helped find sources who knew him during his most difficult days, regardless of what they had to say about him.

Other sources, located through standard reporting techniques, were essential to fill in gaps in Howard's memory and to provide perspective. The result is not an "as told to" memoir. Conversations are reconstructed to the best of Howard's recollection, supported whenever possible by the memory of other participants, court transcripts or published reports.

All events and characters are real. Two names, Roger Stark and Benjamin LeParre, are aliases.

Howard Finkelstein talking to client Octavious Williams in court.
Photograph *The Miami Herald,* April 5, 1990

An Introduction

Murder finally drew me to Howard Finkelstein.

I'd been reading about him for years, as had everyone in South Florida. Howard the ponytailed public defender was almost as much a staple of local news in the 1970s and '80s as hurricanes and carjacked tourists.

For Howard, every case was a cause and every cause was consuming. Depending on your politics, he could be lovable or irritable. Regardless, he was quotable. As the assignment editor in the Miami Herald's bureau in Fort Lauderdale, I knew and appreciated that more than most.

Reporters always came back from an interview excited, not just about what Howard had said but about Howard. He was witty and charming, and his views were a perfect match for a generation of journalists inspired as much by Woodstock as Watergate.

Howard was celebrated for his rousing defense of people who were being swept aside along with the old beach bars, seashell shacks and mom-and-pop motels.

As long as Howard was fighting for the poor against a system we all distrusted, we couldn't help seeing him as a hero. We missed the bigger story, when Howard stopped fighting for the poor and started fighting himself. We didn't start paying attention again until Howard stopped fighting altogether— when Howard nearly died.

We missed the story because what happened to Howard was happening to so many people everywhere, including some of the people who were writing about him, that there didn't seem to be anything unusual.

Howard got hooked on cocaine.

In South Florida in the early 1980s, that was like saying someone had become hooked on bowling: Not everyone did, but everyone knew someone who did. You didn't stop inviting these people to your house, even if they made you a little nervous every time they went into the bathroom

We know better now, some of us anyway, because of what cocaine did to Howard and so many others. It transformed an admirably decent and generous man into a self-absorbed, self-destructive wreck. The defender became a defendant.

Howard came as close to utter ruin as any human can. So did his wife, Donna. This is also her story, and the story of many others like her.

The details of Howard's downfall can wait a few pages because this story will mean more if you know the ending: Howard not only survived, he became a better man, a better husband and a loving father.

I finally met Howard in the spring of 1990, after I traded my city editor's office for a reporter's notepad. I was covering a murder. It was Howard's first case in three years, since he quit cocaine. He won it without going to trial by showing that the police had arrested the wrong man.

I arranged an interview, expecting Howard to deliver an exultant speech. Even in the dim light of the old courthouse hallway I recognized him immediately by the ponytail. I could not have identified him by his words.

He spoke softly, humbly about his good work. I was impressed by his humility not only because it surprised me but because it seemed so sincere. I knew about Howard's problems—everyone knew about Howard's problems—but I wondered if he had recovered something more important than his license to practice law.

Howard seemed genuinely pleased that I asked. Sitting on a long bench in that narrow hall, Howard told me a story unlike anything I'd heard or read before. Other former addicts blame drugs for their problems, credit God or their analysts for saving them and offer their stock portfolios as proof of their salvation.

Howard didn't see himself as a man whose life was ruined by cocaine. Howard saw himself as a man who ruined his own life and took cocaine to pretend he hadn't.

Howard's story wasn't just about addiction and recovery. It was about a man who came to care too much about foolish pleasures, and about himself. The proof of his ruination wasn't a lost job or a lost home but his lost ideals. The proof of his redemption, he said, would lie in what he could do for others.

He had his health back, but it was more important to him that he'd regained his sense of purpose. As long as he held it, he said, he had nothing to fear from cocaine—and he was determined to hold it with all his might.

The people close to Howard

Donna Chase — The college classmate Howard married

Maury Finkelstein — Howard's father

Andy Mavrides — Howard's teacher and role model

Ed Stack — The sheriff Howard battled

Barry "The Bear" Hunwick — The accused hitman Howard feared

Little Ray Thompson — The drug dealer Howard defended

Judy Stern — The friend and secretary who tried to save Howard

Andy Mavrides
1976

Ed Stack
May 12, 1982

Barry Hunwick
June 11, 1982

Little Ray Thompson
April 19, 1986

Kelly	The young love Howard hurt
Alan Schreiber	The public defender who gave Howard a second chance
Roger Stark	The drug dealer who haunted Howard
Harry Gulkin	The judge-turned-lawyer who came to Howard's rescue
Eddie Williams	The innocent man Howard saved
Cynthia Thomas	The AIDS victim Howard befriended

Harry Gulkin
August 14, 1989

Eddie Williams
c. March, 1990

Cynthia Thomas, June 3, 1992

All photographs The Miami Herald

Two Men on Trial

Octavious Williams had no accomplice the night he became a killer. Whatever else was in contention, that much was clear: This strong boy of 17 shot a man in the face and left him in the street to die.

But when the day came in March, 1990 for him to face judge and jury, another man stood trial right beside Octavious. That's what caused the fuss.

Through weeks of pretrial motions, the sort of routine recitation of legal precedents and boilerplate objections that even lawyers and judges often yawn through, the swinging doors of room 910 at the Broward County Courthouse in Fort Lauderdale, Florida, had been flapping furiously as heads popped in, craning and nodding toward the shorter, older man.

They came from every corner of the old courthouse along the New River: judges, lawyers, prosecutors, bailiffs, clerks, reporters. They all just happened to be passing by, the way people happen to pass by terrible accident scenes that they hear about on the radio. They wanted to see if Howard Finkelstein was really back, and if there was anything left of him.

In a very real sense, the trial of Octavious Williams had become the trial of his lawyer.

Long before Octavious ever learned to walk or talk, Howard was the star of this courthouse. The reporters and cameras were always waiting when Howard emerged from court, victorious. He won spectacular cases in spectacular fashion. He captivated juries with emotional pleas and dramatic shows. Time and again he overturned laws that had been used to punish people who had no money or power.

Now Howard needed to prove that he could do these things again, sober.

When the bailiff called Octavious' name, the defendant stood straight up. Then he turned toward the jurors and smiled, ever so gently. He looked so nice, so straight-backed and short-haired and polite, that he might have been waiting to receive a civics award at a high school assembly instead of standing trial for second-degree murder. It was all Howard's idea, every gesture and tic.

Howard smiled at the jurors, too, but that was natural. Howard smiled at everyone, always. But this time, he wanted the jurors to see past his smile. He turned his head so they could see the ponytail draped halfway down the back of his blue suit—sandy, fluffy, shining beneath the overhead lights. For all that had changed about Howard over the years, the ponytail had not and he was certain it never would.

"You may not like this," he said, "but please, please don't hold it against my client. This is mine."

When the jurors smiled back, Howard began to relax, just a little, for the first time that day. Howard had always believed he devoted every bit of his energy and intelligence to his client, but he would not be human if he hadn't been thinking just a little about himself, about how important this case was to him, about everything that had happened in the four years since his own arrest and in the years that led to it. The anxiety showed the moment he woke up that morning. Howard's fingers immediately poked at his belly.

This was the habit Howard had fallen into, and he made no apologies. Of all the habits he'd made and broken, this one was nothing to worry about, nothing that could kill him or anyone else. Without a second thought, or even a first, Howard's fingers pressed at the thin, elastic skin and the muscles, just below, that had become hard as bone. He needed to be sure that no fat had settled in during the night.

Howard did this automatically, whether he was awakened by anxiety at 3 a.m. or a crying daughter at 4 a.m. or the alarm at 5. Howard felt his belly and then walked out onto the patio, into the Florida heat, to spread his back against the rough concrete.

Howard knows the routine without thinking: he locks his hands behind his head and pulls his nose to his knees. Then he swings his head back to the ground. If there is any doubt in his fingertips, the slightest suspicion of fat, he does 100 more. Then the real exercise begins.

For at least an hour, Howard lifts and stretches his legs and arms, and then turns to the weights. He stands and raises 90 pounds of cold iron to his chin, then pushes it as far up as his arms can reach. Howard weighs 120 pounds. When he is done, when he is nearly exhausted, he runs.

Howard runs at least five miles through quiet, shaded streets, past the homes of neighbors whose greatest fear is that the people Howard cares most about will move next door.

Between the time he quit cocaine and the day he returned to the courtroom as a lawyer, Howard had been squeezing the fat from his body, especially the belly fat that other lawyers lay proudly over their belts and bundle in silk vests. Howard is not like other lawyers. He does not share their greed and they do not share his anger. They could never be so angry with themselves.

Howard had been angry since he was a child. By high school, he was angry with his parents and his teachers and his country. He was angry about war and racism and poverty and the unfairness of life. He decided to fight. Howard fought long and well and he heard applause that made him fight harder. He did not realize that he was fighting himself until it was very nearly too late.

Howard did not realize because he could not see. When he decided to fight, he closed his eyes and he did not open them for nearly 20 years. Howard was a good man who closed his eyes and got lost.

At 38, he was still lost, but at least he knew it and he knew where he dared never go again. And if he was still punishing himself, at least there was no illusion and no mistake.

It is better to sweat and beat and starve the fat from his belly than to be sweated and beaten and starved by cocaine.

Howard loved cocaine more than he loved his wife and his mother. He is ashamed of that, even though he knows it happened to so many others before and that it still happens every day. He is ashamed because cocaine unmasked him, and he could no longer believe he was different. Howard is ashamed because he is merely human and utterly powerless against the greater force that propels us all.

Howard has always tried, harder than most, but he was still too angry—and too scared—when he returned to the courtroom to forgive his failures. For a long time, he tried to forget them, to wish they didn't happen, to believe that they could be erased. He still cannot remember the crash that almost stole his life and family.

He remembers only that it was another awful night in an awful week of the most awful time of his life.

He was not drunk. Howard was rarely drunk. He had no use for alcohol when he could get cocaine, and he could always get cocaine—and Percodan, and Dilaudid, and anything else he wanted.

Howard had money and he had friends. It was the best part of being a lawyer.

That is what really frightens Howard, even today—that having money and friends enough to buy drugs had become the best part of being a lawyer. He understands why men sell their souls, but he cannot understand why he simply abandoned his, left it lying somewhere like an old coat, and walked away.

Howard has always been afraid of men with no souls, and sure he would never be one. He saw what these men did to other men, to poor men and women and children who had no one to defend them. When he was very young and very full of energy and ideals, he decided that he would fight such men for all the others.

He understood the cost, he thought. He knew he would be cursed and kicked and beaten as often as he won. He knew he would never be rich. But he could never be happy doing anything else, and if there was anything selfish about Howard, it was that he wanted to be happy.

And he wanted to be liked.

He could endure the curses of the powerful as long as he heard the cheers of the weak. He could stand being kicked now and then if it meant being lifted high and kissed by the people he cared most about.

He lived with hate because he wanted love, and he found it, more than he ever imagined. In time, even people who should have hated him loved him. He was so passionate, so intelligent, so dogged in his defense of people everyone else abandoned that even the judges and policemen and prosecutors he fought so hard came to like having him around.

It helped that he was so cute. What harm could there be in this little man who smiled all the time?

When he was young, he was adorable, an elfin hippie with a pony tail bouncing down his back. When he was older, when the drugs began to show on his face, he was cuter still, looking weary from his good fights but still eager to show his pinch-faced smile.

People forgave Howard because they liked him so much. They forgave his excesses as well as his trespasses. He wishes they hadn't. He wishes now that someone had made him understand soon enough that he had come to care too much about himself, before he came so close to losing everything.

His wife, Donna, would have told him, but she didn't know until it was too late. And then, when she tried, he cursed her. As much as she loved him, he wouldn't listen, and that nearly killed her.

A lot of other people knew, but if they tried to tell him, they didn't try hard enough. Or they didn't see what they didn't want to see, and that is hardest for Howard to understand. He even left his crack pipe on the desk in his office, maybe because he wanted someone to stop him. It was always there when he came back.

If Howard had screamed at the top of his lungs, he couldn't have done much more to get attention in those six weeks before the crash. By then he knew what was wrong, but it was too late to just walk away. He had been trying to quit for a year, tried every weekend as Donna begged him, bullied him, threw his drugs in the trash.

Howard came home high every Friday, crashed by Saturday, and flew into a sweating, choking rage by Sunday.

And every Monday, Howard bought more cocaine. He mixed it with baking soda and cooked it into rocks on Donna's stove while she cried. He left home, and came back. Donna left, and came back too. She finally came to believe that if he could not quit cocaine she could not live with him, and if he could not stop lying, she could not live at all.

If they could only get away, she thought, it would be easier. If Howard didn't go to work, he could make the weekend last until he didn't need cocaine any more. He agreed, and they flew to Aruba. Howard didn't know anyone there, and Donna felt safe.

Howard wasn't in Aruba a half-hour before he bought cocaine. It wasn't hard to find. He could see people just like himself, all around.

Howard doesn't remember what happened when he got back from Aruba, but he remembers not caring anymore whether he quit—not caring anymore whether he lived or died.

He had been close to death more than once during these drug years. He had been threatened, he had been shot at. Once he crashed his car, blind on cocaine, and was lucky to crawl away. The police recognized him as the funny hippie lawyer and gave him a break.

Two Broward County sheriff's deputies, Engels and Brown, finally gave Howard the break he needed at 8:27 p.m., July 2, 1987. They marked Howard down as arrest LH870461: possession of cocaine, possession of oxycodone, possession of hydromorphone, driving under the influence and possession of drug paraphernalia.

They did not cite Howard for the U-turn. The U-turn is why Howard does not refer to the crash as an accident. He had no reason to turn back unless he wanted to hit the police car.

There were three of them parked in front of the house on NW 56th Avenue in Lauderhill, Florida, one city away from Howard's home in Plantation. The deputies were investigating a robbery. Howard does not remember why he was driving down that street.

The police told him later that he hit the brakes just before the right front fender of his 1984 Cadillac Eldorado punched into the side of patrol unit 792. Howard's Cadillac embarrassed him almost as much as the crash and the drugs. Why was he driving a car built for men he hated?

Howard doesn't think he was hurt, but he doesn't remember that either. He complained later that his back hurt, that he couldn't walk and stretch and touch his nose the way the officers wanted him to. He wonders now if it was just another excuse, if the lawyer in him was trying to build a defense while the addict was trying to surrender.

Howard remembers this: He was as polite as the deputies were surprised. They were startled by this thunderous intrusion, and by the long-haired lawyer who told them where to find his drugs.

Stumbling and swaying, Howard waived all objections to a search. The deputies looked under the white leather seat and found a half-dozen loose Dilaudid pills, one Percodan, and a six-inch rolled pipe made of aluminum foil that Howard had used to smoke crack. Driving the way he did, driving with these drugs in the car, was enough to send him to jail, at least for the night, and Howard knew that, so he asked the deputies to do him a favor.

Howard asked them to get his briefcase from the trunk. Howard could not go anywhere for the night without his briefcase. That's where he kept most of his drugs.

The deputies opened the briefcase and found a fat bottle of pills with the label torn off and a plastic bag containing cocaine. If the deputies hadn't opened the briefcase, Howard would have faced nothing more serious than misdemeanor charges; now police had enough evidence to charge him with felonies.

Howard would have to go to jail without his briefcase; he could stay there a very long time because of it.

There was nothing cute about Howard when they took him to jail. The police took a picture, his booking mug, with his mouth twisted open and eyes swelled shut. He looks dead. It looks like a photo of a corpse pulled from a river, the kind of picture police carry from place to place asking if anyone knew the victim.

Howard cannot bear to look at this picture, because he knows who the real victims were and who they might have been. He knows he could have killed someone that night and that if that had happened, it would have killed him.

He knows that because of him, Donna, wanted to kill herself. He knows that if she succeeded, their daughters would never have been born. He does not know how many others would have died, or might as well have.

Howard wasn't just another lawyer with a drug problem. He was the only one who could keep a kid like Octavious from going to jail for life. There were other lawyers willing, maybe other lawyers smarter, but it would be damn hard to find a smarter lawyer willing to fight the way Howard did for so little money.

Even at his worst, even in the high times when he sold his mind and voice to violent men and cash fell freely from his pockets, Howard always made time to help the poor. He promised himself and Donna that he always would, but the drug addict in the corpse photo could not keep that promise. Even if he lived, even if he became well again, it wasn't likely he would still be a lawyer.

Sick at heart, sick to his stomach, Howard stopped fighting, at least for a while.

"I'm going to plead guilty," he told the cop, still smiling, head politely tilted downward, as videotape recorded his wobbly attempts to walk a straight line.

Howard fell backward as he tried to pull his stocking feet, one at a time, off the white line on the floor. He could not pull against the weight of all the drugs from all the years when Howard believed he was above all this.

Hours passed, but Howard still had trouble standing. He looked like a sick little boy, talking low and trying so hard to please. At 12:31 a.m., Howard Finkelstein, 5-foot-3, 123 pounds, blue eyes, light brown hair, white and male, was officially charged and allowed to use the phone. He called Donna and told her that he was in jail.

"Thank God," she said, but Howard didn't understand.

Howard was only dimly aware of what had happened that night, but he knew instinctively where he was when the drug haze finally let him peek through. He had been to the Broward County Jail many times to visit clients. It was right behind the courthouse where he worked. He knew all the deputies, all the guards. He knew that all he had to do was call through the door when it was time to go and the buzzer would sound and he would walk down the corridor, through the common room, past the security desk and out the front door. He did not know where his client could have gone. He did not know why he was there alone.

Howard called to the guards, and no one came. He called louder and pulled at the door, hard.

"It must be broken," he thought, and he passed out, again.

In the belly of the '60s

Howard tried to hide his belly.

When he was very young, it didn't matter. He grew up in a small town in an old state where there were lots of chubby little boys and chubby old men and chubby women of all ages, and no one cared.

But when he was older and he moved to the new place, to Florida, where everyone lived at the beach and everyone was thin and tan and tall, Howard tried to hide a belly that no one else noticed, and he wished he could hide the rest. When he moved to Florida, Howard found out how different he was. He didn't like that at all.

Until he moved to Florida, in his sophomore year of high school, Maurice Finkelstein's oldest child was perfect.

He was polite and funny and smart. He played Little League baseball, and he played the game as hard, and as well, as he studied. There was something warm and nice about this boy that made grownups turn toward him and go to him and talk to him. There could be a hundred children behind him at lunchtime, but the cafeteria lady would stop the line to tell Howard about her grandchildren.

So many strangers stopped Howard to ask for the time or to ask for directions or just to say hello that he decided he glowed. Howard thought there was a light shining out of his head, and he liked that. It could not be a halo, because he had not earned a halo, but there was light and it drew others to him, until he lost it.

When Howard was a boy, he shined his light in a small town

and ran with all his might around the bases and he idolized his father.

Howard's father believed in hard work and hard play as the best antidotes for a hard life. He did not let the Depression stand in the way of his education and he would not let misfortune block the way for others. Maurice Finkelstein, Ph.D., grew up to be a social worker.

All the while Howard was growing up, he listened to Maury talk about society's obligations to the poor and watched him carry through. Maury raised money for a Jewish community center, then became its director. In those days, before Howard was different, his family lived in a tract house like a hundred others and Howard was happy.

Howard fit in that little town, two hours north of New York City, but he wondered if he would fit anywhere else. When Howard was done playing for the day, he came home and watched the news on television, and he wondered why the rest of America seemed so angry. Binghamton was nothing like the angry America that Howard watched on the news, the America of race riots and college riots, of peace protests and hippies fighting the police. Howard wondered about that America. He wanted to see it, but he wasn't sure he wanted to live there.

Curiosity sent him there for the weekend soon after he turned 16. On Aug. 16, 1969, without saying a word, Howard walked out to the main road and hitched an hour's ride down Route 17 to Bethel, to his epiphany. He was startled to see them, thousands of them, marching through the alfalfa field. They were the ones on television, the ones with long hair who smoked marijuana as casually as they breathed and threw off their clothes to celebrate the sun. Howard stretched out on the soft ground and let his mind dance to the music of Woodstock.

Howard was different when he hiked out of the bog and ruin of what had been Max Yasgur's farm. He had lived with freaks for three days in a wet and crowded place without enough food or water or toilets, a place that his parents and their friends could not stand for an hour, and he watched the hippies sing and dance and share whatever they had. If there was anger in America, Howard thought, it was not coming from these people.

Howard does not know whether he could have been happy in his little town after that. At summer's end, his father took a job as director of a Jewish community center in Florida and the family moved to Hollywood, a beachside town halfway between Miami and Fort Lauderdale. It was a place that did not make Howard feel welcome, a place that was never meant for him.

A man named Joseph Young first imagined this city in the boom days of the 1920s. It was all mangrove and marsh then, not much good for farming. But the rail line cut straight through, and there was a natural cove to be dredged for a seaport. Young looked at that mangrove and marsh and he saw paradise, and money.

He hired men to drain and strip and fill the land, and architects to weave royal palms with barrel-tile roofs and roughstone courtyards. They built a park in a circle in the middle of town, and a bandshell. Hollywood would be a city for both the idle rich and the merchants who served them. But most of all, it would be a city with charm to turn the tourist's heads, and open their wallets.

Like much of Florida, it was a charm of illusion, of perfect weather and endless ease. The finest homes would stand high on Hollywood Hills, looking down to the sea. There are no hills in South Florida, just a rise of eight or 10 feet at the coastal ridge, but the tour-bus drivers all followed Mr. Young's instructions and shifted into low gear as they approached. Passengers gasped as the engine strained, and agreed that the view was magnificent. The biggest worry for Young's salesmen was running out of ink.

Then it was over, like that. The hurricane of 1926 washed away the illusion, and Young went broke. Not much changed in Hollywood for a long time, until the families came in the 1950s. The end of World War II brought a new boom to Florida, and new illusions. By the time Howard's family arrived in 1969, there were 100,000 people in Hollywood and most of them lived in tract houses, like the ones in upstate New York, but without basements or attics. Maury and Charlotte Finkelstein and their children, Howard, 16, Susan, 13, and Ricky, 6, settled into an apartment near the beach while the contractor finished building their new house, in Hollywood Hills.

Howard hated the beach. He hated wearing a bathing suit, although his parents could not see why, because they could not see the belly that felt bigger and uglier every day. Baby fat wasn't such a big deal up North, where it was wrapped deep in heavy shirts and coats most of the year. But Howard learned new rules in Florida, at South Broward High School: In Florida, everyone is supposed to be tall and trim and tanned. If you aren't, no one will like you, and nothing ever hurt Howard more than not being liked.

Howard came to Florida and cried. For the first time in his life, Howard had no friends and that scared him. He could not make friends unless he could be like everyone else, and he couldn't do that. He could not change his body, although he tried. Howard had always played hard, as his father wanted, and now he played harder. He went to gym class and took the little-fat-boy taunts and practiced his baseball. Somehow, he would fit in, because he had to.

As far as he knew, the rest of his family was happy in Florida. His parents were making friends, and his father had found a second home at the Hollywood Playhouse. Always a showman, Maury had become a seasoned director of amateur theater, and Hollywood offered an abundance of talent. There was one actor who stood out, a teacher named Andrew Mavrides. He was a Greek and he had the soul of a Greek, the soul of the ancient theater. His voice was as deep as the creases in his face. Andy could be funny or angry or witty or hurtful, but he could never be ignored. No matter the role, Andy Mavrides was Hollywood's star, and he soon became Howard's.

Teaching gave Andy an audience every day, and a paycheck while he went to law school at night. In his late 30s, Andy aspired to the twin theaters of law and politics, and the classroom gave him an opportunity to rehearse for both.

MAV/RIDES! That's what he wrote on the board the first day of class. At least one student smiled: Howard Finkelstein. He liked everything about Andy, right away. He liked Andy's beard and the peace sign hanging around his neck and the thick, silver-streaked hair that curled toward his shoulders. Howard knew immediately that Andy was different from other teachers, that he had never learned the adult's fear of being noticed.

"This class is called humanities," Andy said. "But it is really about man's inhumanity to man."

All through the year, Andy talked about race and greed and power and poverty. He talked about Vietnam, and he wanted his students to talk back. He did not demand that they agree with him or their parents or the government. He demanded that they think, and he gave them ideas to think about. Andy's ideas did not all come from textbooks. Some came from Marx, and Eldridge Cleaver. Not everyone liked Andy's ideas, or even his beard. The principal told him to cut it off, but Andy wouldn't do it. The principal backed down.

Howard loved listening to Andy. He read all the books Andy talked about, and stayed after class to ask questions. He even followed Andy home to ask more. There was no place Howard fit better than Andy's class except Andy's home. No one gave him more attention and no one offered more praise. When Maury left, Howard still had Andy.

Six months after they moved to Florida, Howard's father moved out. Howard has heard, over and over, what his father says about that time and what his mother says about that time and he still doesn't know the truth. Maury moved to Miami Beach for a while, then to Atlanta. He gave up fund raising and social work and everything Howard thought was important and decided, for the first time, to try making money. It took years for Howard to understand that. He still thinks Maury was wrong.

For the first time in his life, Howard began making judgments about right and wrong. With Andy and his books as guide, Howard plotted the whole world into rights and wrongs, with angry and depressing finality. Howard left little room for doubt or hope or redemption. Sometime in his last two years of high school, Howard decided the world was going to hell. If there was any brightness at all in Howard's vision, other than Andy, it was the discovery that there were others who felt the same way.

Howard likes to say that he is a child of the '60s, but he was born a bit too late for that: July 31, 1953. He is more like a flower child's younger brother who tried on hand-me-down tie-dyes and bell bottoms and suddenly felt older and wiser. The generation celebrated in Hair, the generation that marched for freedom in the South and wrestled police in Chicago and prayed to Hindu gods in California, was already passing into adulthood. Some had even grown up. But their clothes and language and politics were new magic to Howard. The longer his hair grew, the more he talked about revolution, the more friends he made.

They would meet after school in the park named for Joseph Young, behind the bandshell, and smoke marijuana. Howard does not remember when he started, but he remembers this: He had plenty of company. If Hollywood had seemed so straight and quiet and sober, it was a lesson in false appearances. His new friends all lived in four-bedroom, one-story homes that were perfect for sleepover guests. Most of the sleepovers were other friends' parents, who swapped partners as casually as they played tennis.

Parental hypocrisy was a major topic of discussion wherever Howard and his friends gathered, behind the bandshell or in Howard's orange VW van or at the pizza parlor that did not sell pizza. Howard and his friends went there to buy LSD. For the sake of appearance, a pizza was always ordered from a real restaurant down the street. Howard remembers eating pizza and LSD, and believing he could hear the walls breathe.

They also listened to music, to Dylan and The Who and Jimi Hendrix. They formed a band, and when the city held a talent show, they sang the winning song. It was a protest song, a protest against drugs. Howard is certain the judges got the joke. He was dating two of them. Howard fit with these people, with their music and their drugs, but he did not fit with everyone.

As a ballplayer, he understood the concept of choosing sides but he did not realize until his senior year in high school that it applied to life. To the principal, to most teachers, to other students, to some of their own parents, Howard and his friends were oddballs at best and dangerous pollutants at worst.

For a while, Howard liked the idea. He liked the attention, and he liked the feeling that he knew something that most didn't. He liked it fine until he realized he had to choose, and he realized the cost. He knew it when the golf team made the papers. Two of the players, two of Howard's closest friends, refused to get a hair cut, and the coach cut them from the roster. Howard thought about this constantly as his growing ponytail bobbed behind his baseball cap.

Howard had become a fine shortstop. He was maturing, if not growing, and as he lost weight he gained speed to match the sureness of his glove. No one doubted that Howard had the range and reflexes to cover more ground than anyone else in school. Maury came back to watch Howard practice, and cheered him on.

"You are good enough to play for the Yankees someday," he told his son, and Howard believed him. But Howard didn't want to play for the Yankees, and as he looked around at the tall boys with crew cuts, he realized that he didn't want to play at all. One day, in the middle of practice, Howard walked off the field and never returned.

At 17, Howard felt he was making the decisive choice of his life. It didn't make him happy, but it made him feel right. If the world was going to hell, Howard wasn't going to be shagging flies when it got there. He was going to be marching in the first wave of damned souls, smoking a joint and carrying a picket sign. His attitude did not endear him to the people who ran South Broward High School.

More and more, Howard made impromptu speeches and handed out leaflets and organized protests against the Vietnam War, the draft, the school dress code. More and more, Howard was sent to the principal's office for a lecture and a paddling. It was legal to paddle students in Florida, a provision that angers Howard far more today than it did then. Then, Howard took his beatings as rite of sacrifice, as validation of the cause.

Howard let the principal slam him across the rear end time and again for more than a year before he decided to strike back. It was legal to paddle students, but not to damage them, and Howard knew that because Andy told him. One day when the paddle slapped home, Howard fell to the floor and screamed.

"You hit my spine!"

He shouted and he rolled and groaned. The principal dropped his paddle and never hit Howard again.

Andy helped Howard see the real lesson: money rules. The moment the principal started to worry about a lawsuit, about his job, he backed down. So forget reason, Andy said. Find a way to cost the other side money, and you will win every time.

Howard didn't know what to make of this. He didn't know where a school got money, much less how to take it away. Then Andy explained. Schools get money from the state for each student. Take away students, even for a while, and the school loses money. Howard understood. He organized a student strike to change the dress code. It lasted one day before the principal gave in.

Bolder now, Howard decided to run for school office. He doesn't remember how he picked vice president of the senior class, but it doesn't matter. The idea was to run, to get attention, not to win. Howard got attention from the start. He would be allowed to make a campaign speech, but only after submitting it for approval, the principal told him. Howard ran to Andy.

"Show him the speech," Andy advised, "but follow your conscience."

Howard submitted a good and proper speech, but delivered the one he had in mind all along. He called his fellow students to action, and they responded immediately. They ran into the halls and through the classrooms, shouting for revolution. The principal called the police.

Three students were hauled off to the police station, and Howard took off after them, hair streaming out the side of his orange van. Others followed, and Howard led a spontaneous march on city hall, demanding that they all be arrested. The police let everyone go.

Howard won the election, but he had lost any sense of purpose in going to school. He read, but he never studied. He argued, but he rarely listened, except to Andy. He was bright enough to pass, but little more. He considered quitting, but Andy told him not to. Andy quit school at 17 and it was years before he went back to get his diploma, and years after that before he went to college, and years after that, while he was teaching to pay the rent, that he went to law school.

"If you quit," Andy said, "they win."

Besides, Howard was meant to go to college. His parents told him so all his life. An encouraging letter from his guidance counselor helped him get into the University of South Florida in Tampa, a few hours from home, which seemed the minimum acceptable distance. With Maury gone, Howard was no more comfortable at home than he was in school, no more in sympathy with his mother than with his principal.

During his senior year in high school, Howard stayed out late nearly every night and always came home drunk or high. His mother would scream and Howard would scream back. They stopped screaming just long enough for Howard to graduate. His mother sat in the audience as Howard stood in line to get his diploma, smoking a joint.

Howard and his friend David went to Atlanta that summer to stay with Maury, who was promoting a mobile-home development. Howard's father did not object to his hair, his drugs or his absence for days at a time. Howard did not object to Maury living with David's mother. Maury told Howard he was proud of him, and expected big things in college. Howard said he expected to go to prison. He was certain he'd lose his college deferment and get drafted. He would never go to Vietnam.

"You could go to Canada," Maury said.

"No," Howard said. "That would be running away."

So he went to college to major in political science in the fall of 1971, three years after Richard Nixon was elected President, four years before the fall of Saigon, and he waited for the draft lottery. Howard was number 265, more than 100 numbers past any possibility of being called. Howard would have to find another fight.

Even in Tampa, on the tranquil Gulf Coast of Florida, Howard found Black Panther rallies and anti-war demonstrations. He also found a political science professor whose impatience with the world matched Howard's, even if his views didn't. The professor cheered the war that Howard hated, but he also cheered Howard for arguing so hard and well.

Howard leaped to the top of that class and rode it as though it were a stallion. There was one student who approached Howard's ability to express ideas, and she disliked him for that as much as she admired him. But Howard paid no attention to Donna Chase, tall and blonde and striking.

Donna had followed her boyfriend to Florida from New Jersey, where she grew up in the very middle-class town of West Orange. Back there, the boys followed Donna. She was always smart enough to be the best at anything she wanted, but she was less interested in scholarship than cheerleading. Donna was a classic Scandinavian beauty who had been adopted as a baby into a Jewish home. She grew up loved and pampered and wonderfully secure, until her father's business went under. It was clear to Donna that he was a victim, that others had taken advantage of his generosity, but he never complained. It is best to be decent and kind, he taught her, even if you are broke.

After her father, other men disappointed Donna. She wondered if she disappointed them. She broke off with the boyfriend from New Jersey shortly after arriving at school, and began to work hard at learning. Finkelstein and the professor both made her angry, Finkelstein because he was so smart, and so obviously aware of it, and the professor because he said women weren't meant for political science.

It is as true now as then: Tell Donna Chase she can't do something, and she will do it, and the one thing she had always done best is get attention. Whenever a question was put to the class, Donna was first to respond. She showed, time and again, that she was studious, thoughtful and persuasive. Then, when she was done, it was Howard's turn. Donna is five inches taller than Howard, but he always made her feel small.

There was no dress code, no principal, no paddle. Even the professors smoked dope. He finished his freshman year on the dean's list and drove home for the summer. The screaming resumed as soon as he arrived.

Howard was absorbed in his own vision of the world when he went away to school, and its focus was even stronger when he returned. He was not interested in his mother's ideas of propriety or sobriety, and he told her so. He would not submit to her authority, and he would not take her money.

Howard hadn't taken money from his mother or his father since they moved to Florida. He was not a spoiled brat, and he was not a hypocrite. Howard understood the value of a dollar better than most, but he did not share it. He wanted no more than he needed to live, and smoke, and he would owe no more in return than a day's work.

When Howard was in high school, he washed pots in a restaurant every afternoon and carried concrete blocks for construction workers all through the summer. He washed enough pots and carried enough blocks to buy the old Volkswagen van for $300 from a kid down the street, and that was all he needed, except a few T-shirts and rolling papers, until he went to college. He did not have the money to pay for college, and he would not ask his mother or his father. He would not take their money if they offered. Howard took out student loans to pay tuition, and he slept in his van when he ran out of money to pay for a room.

Howard slept in his van and ate what he could afford. Sometimes he ate dog food. When he came home from his first year of college, Howard could not afford to waste all his time arguing with his mother, because he needed to make money.

He began making nightly trips to golf courses to dive for lost balls in the lakes.

He sold them the next day for 10 cents each, and on a good night, he could make $30 before he went off to join his friends. When he was in high school, Howard came home at all hours high on drugs. Now he came home at all hours high on drugs and soaking wet.

One night he came home and found everything he owned piled on the front lawn. He left it all there and drove away. He did not speak to his mother again for 10 years.

Zen in the '70s

It never occurred to Howard that his principal might have been right about anything. It did not occur to Howard, for a very, very long time, that his mother might have done the wrong thing for a good reason, because she was so hurt.

He read about Eastern religions, about Zen and Taoism, and marveled at the concept of balance in man and nature. But he never stopped, even for a moment, to look for balance in his own life. He read Kerouac and felt joined with the generation that explored the road, but it never occurred to him to explore, too.

Once Howard had found his own road, his path of righteousness, he ran as fast as he could and never looked up, or to this side or that. Or behind. He came to trust his path so much, to know it so well, that he could run with his eyes closed, and he did. The longer he ran, the more he believed.

The path carried him through fear and anger, through anxiety and depression. By the time it carried him through college, Howard breathed the giddy smugness of a long-distance runner. The war was over, Nixon resigned, and Howard had survived both. He followed Andy to law school, and believing opened the door.

His college grades were so much better than high school's that he graduated with honors, but he could not make up for all the lessons lost. Howard's law board scores were marginal, at best. But he wrote an essay that helped persuade the

University of Miami to give him a chance. He argued that law was a tool for change, for others, for the better, and asked for the chance to learn how to use it. He got the chance, and he learned quickly.

Howard learned all day, and he learned more at night. He followed Andy and his friend Alcee Hastings and others as they hacked their new path through the old political woods of Fort Lauderdale and made a little clearing to oil and aim their cannon. Howard would carry the ammunition, or the water, just to be there. He wanted, more than anything, to carry the banner.

When the men Howard followed formed a chapter of the American Civil Liberties Union, Howard volunteered to help, and he was as helpful as a law student could be. Howard answered phones and ran errands and looked up lawsuits. It wasn't long before he joined one.

Howard was still in law school when he sued the sheriff of Broward County.

Ed Stack was a powerful and popular man, with a powerful and popular cause: public decency. He was always campaigning, and always on that same theme. He had no use, he said, for the filth mongers who were trying to destroy his community. He had no use for pornographers or pimps, or women who danced naked, and he would run them out of town.

Howard knew he wouldn't. Howard knew the pornographers and pimps and women who danced naked had come to town long before Ed Stack and they would not leave until everyone else did. Even Howard the young socialist did not doubt that supply would meet demand, and he knew the demand was tremendous. What was South Florida without sin?

The real gold along the Gold Coast was first mined by rum runners, and the tourists were drawn by back-room casinos and beachside bordellos a half-century before discount air fares and spring break. It was no coincidence that Al Capone once spent his winters there, or that mobsters like Tony Provenzano still did. Howard did not believe this law-and-order sheriff could change that, or that he really wanted to. What Ed Stack really wanted from his morality campaign were votes, and he got plenty of them, even from those good parents who swapped partners at night.

Howard was less appalled by hypocrisy than tactics. Stack sent his deputies to stores that sold dirty books or magazines or tapes and ordered them to stop everyone who went in. The cops parked out front with their lights flashing, asked the customers for identification, wrote down license plate numbers, and warned anyone who still insisted on going inside that there could be trouble. The intent was clear: to chase away the customers and to keep people from seeing or reading anything Ed Stack didn't like.

Howard decided to become the customer that couldn't be chased.

Howard Finkelstein, smart-ass law school student, drove to the Ace Adult Book Store on West Broward Boulevard, just outside Fort Lauderdale, and took notes as he took the deputies' abuse. The deputies who usually gave warnings got one in return, and this one was real. With Howard as both witness and victim, the ACLU filed suit in federal court to stop the sheriff from harassing the bookstores.

A judge ordered the sheriff to leave the stores alone, but the sheriff didn't back down. If the law wouldn't allow him to close these places, then he wanted a new law, and Sheriff Stack was accustomed to getting what he wanted.

When Howard picked on Ed Stack for his first public fight, he picked on a heavyweight. Stack had the power that came from running the biggest political patronage machine in the county. He also had the brains to use it. He may have acted like an old Southern sheriff, and talked like one when it suited him, but Stack was a former law professor from New York who had became a master politician in his mid-60s.

He was a Republican in a Democratic state, but that turned in his favor when Goldwater claimed the South while losing everywhere else. Stack had an honest, square-jawed look, with just the right touch of gray streaked through his short, wavy hair. His voice was firm but soft, although he kept his teeth tight together as he talked, as though he was afraid of losing his dentures.

Lewdness ordinance approved, ACLU maintains new law unfair

The Miami Herald reported that the County Commission unanimously approved a law to deny a license to any suspicious business. The story said the audience cheered as Stack promised to use the law to close every massage parlor and topless bar. The story did not report whether anyone cheered Howard Finkelstein, a law student representing the ACLU at the meeting. But it did devote six paragraphs to his objections. The first was that the ordinance was submitted to commissioners right before the meeting, by Stack, with no chance for the public to study it.

Howard did not sway the commission, but he got attention. For more than a year, when the newspapers wrote about Ed Stack and his morality campaign they almost always quoted Howard, too. At 24, he had become a reliable source, journalistic counterpoint to a powerful man.

If Stack noticed Howard, he never said so publicly. He had no reason to object. The louder Howard and the ACLU complained, the more praise Stack won from conservative constituents. And while the county was filling with Democrats who moved from the North, they were older Democrats, not the sort to side with hippies and hookers. They were the sort who welcomed Ed Stack when he switched to their party to run for Congress at the height of his anti-smut campaign.

Stack made morality his cornerstone, and it was a far luckier choice than he could have guessed. It was equally lucky that Stack had failed to make good on his promise to close all the topless bars. Weeks before the election, an elderly man in a suit was arrested after getting into a fistfight at the Centerfold Lounge on Federal Highway. It was Congressman J. Herbert Burke, Stack's opponent.

Burke swore he was conducting his own investigation of naked dancing. Stack won a landslide.

Years later, Howard laughed to think that he may have helped Stack get elected. At the time, he didn't know what to think, except this: He liked the attention. It came at the right time. After all the turmoil of his teens, Howard was comfortable with his life. He was already on his way, by his own measure, to becoming a success.

He was sure now that he would be a lawyer, and lawyers do not eat dog food or live in vans. Howard did not think he could ever ask for more than this: work he believed in, food fit for humans and a roof over his head.

He was thrilled to share his roof with Kelly.

Howard met her at a cousin's bar mitzvah two years before, when she was 19 and he was 23, and they had been living together since. They were the same size, and she was so cute they could have been twins, except that her honey-blonde hair was a little lighter and just a little longer than his.

Kelly and Howard moved into a small, slat-windowed house in the old part of Fort Lauderdale, with two bedrooms and cinder-block walls and a garage in the back yard. The rent was cheap enough, and the landlord was glad to have them. The landlord was Howard's father.

Howard loved Kelly, and he loved to listen to her sing. She sang for him at home while he smoked marijuana, and she sang every night in clubs while he drank beer. In his last year of law school, Howard would bring his books to the bars and study by flashlight. He watched from backstage, mouthing the words and smiling. Howard loved Kelly so much he didn't mind listening to her sing disco. Disco helped pay the bills.

For the first and last time in his life, Howard had nothing to worry about except finding another good fight, and he went looking for it in the Broward Public Defender's Office.

Alan Schreiber had already been running the place for a long time. He was a smart politician who was rarely opposed at election time and won big regardless. Most of the people who voted for him had no idea what he did and would not like it if they found out.

It would strike them as odd, at best, that they were paying so much money for cops and prosecutors to put people in jail, and more money for Schreiber and his assistants to set those same people free.

It even struck some judges and lawyers that way, but few got angry at Schreiber, who rarely attacked or belittled or even complained about the people who ran the system he was paid to fight. Outside court, he was a good Democrat who delivered what his party asked. Inside court, his lawyers won as often as anyone in a day when trials had become obsolete.

Schreiber hired good people and kept them, even though he couldn't pay any better than any other public defender. He had an eye for opportunity. Sometimes, he hired good people who wouldn't get a chance anywhere else because they were a little different or had problems, so they owed him loyalty that exceeded a paycheck.

From everything he heard and read, hiring Howard Finkelstein would be as much an opportunity for his office as it was for this bright young man.

"God, what a mistake," Schreiber said to himself when he saw Howard for the first time. He was so certain of his instincts that he didn't bother to interview Howard before hiring him as an intern. Howard did not dress up for his first day on the job, and he did not cut his hair. Schreiber kicked himself, but he did not kick Howard, and he did not tell him to change. Schreiber had made a commitment and he would keep it as long as Howard kept his. He was not disappointed.

Howard worked as hard at becoming a lawyer as he did at being liked. He took the work he was given, the work no one else wanted, and did it well. When his internship was up, Howard was hired full time. He still got the work no one else wanted, but Howard thought it was terrific. He got all the cases that didn't matter.

The people who came to the public defender's office were all poor, but some had bigger problems than others. Some faced years in prison, accused of murder or rape or robbery, and they got experienced lawyers. Some just needed someone to process the paperwork as they paid fines for littering or loitering, and that was Howard's job.

They were the cases no one wanted and there were plenty of them, almost as many as there were people no one wanted. This was the point of so many laws: to make the people nobody wanted go away.

In the old neighborhoods, nobody wanted the young people who slept on the beach. In the young neighborhoods, nobody wanted the old bums who slept under bridges. In the white neighborhoods, nobody wanted black people to sleep anywhere. Wherever there were people nobody wanted, the police arrested them, lawyers told them to plead guilty and judges took away whatever money they had before warning them not to get caught again.

It had been this way for a long time, all carefully scripted in decades of ordinances. Howard's part was small but important, a role played by so many others before as they learned the ways of court and practiced for bigger parts. It was not a role much noticed outside the courtroom, not a role to be reviewed, much less applauded. Howard changed that.

Howard did not think it should be against the law to be unwanted. He didn't think people volunteered to be unwanted, any more than he did when he was the fat, little new kid in school. In fact, Howard thought the law was upside down. Howard thought law should be used to protect the unwanted—the poor and powerless—from the rest of us. So Howard wrote himself a new role, a bigger role, and found the fight he had been looking for.

Lauderdale 'hobo' laws challenged by attorney

Howard won his first headline by refusing to defend Harold Johnson, 21, against a charge of sleeping in a vacant lot just south of the Las Olas bridge in Fort Lauderdale. Instead, Howard demanded that the city defend its law. He called it unconstitutional, and asked a judge to decide. It was a question County Judge Harry Gulkin had been waiting for.

For a year, Gulkin had watched the long parade of Harold Johnsons from his seat on the bottom rung of the Broward County court system. A successful lawyer from New Jersey who had been on the bench about a year, Gulkin was paying his judicial and political dues in a suburban court annex where the minor cases were shuttled for processing. Young prosecutors and young public defenders brought him hundreds of even-younger defendants, especially when the colleges were on break. Gulkin had no argument with the idea that it was not good to turn every lawn and beach into a free public motel, but he shook his head at the vague and poorly worded law itself:

"It will be unlawful for any person to occupy, lodge, or sleep in the open on private property, in vacant lots, in or under bridges or structures...or upon any public beach between the hours of 6 p.m. and 8 a.m."

What did occupy mean? Was it against the law to stand on a bridge or walk on the beach after 6 p.m.? Was it against the law to fall asleep? Gulkin wondered when some young lawyer would be bright enough, bold enough, to ask. He knew the answer when he saw Howard and his ponytail.

Lauderdale 'sleeping in open' laws struck down.

The judge told the city to open the beach, and it did. That weekend, the bearded, beaded masses snored in peace, from one end to the other. If the city wanted a law, it had to write one that suited the Constitution, the judge ordered. The city attorney and city commission and police chief all agreed.

Howard won more than a court case. He won respect, confidence, and more attention that he ever dreamed. Most important, he won the support of his boss, Alan Schreiber. Howard knows that another politician might have backed away from Howard's fights, or thrown him out, but Schreiber slapped him on the back and said do it again. And Howard did.

Lifeguards lose right of arrest.

For years, until Howard came along, the lifeguards on Fort Lauderdale beach acted like cops. They even carried badges.

One of them arrested Frank McHale, 23, after ordering him to put out a marijuana cigarette. Howard attacked the law giving lifeguards arrest power without requiring them to meet the standards of police officers. A judge was impressed, and Howard won again.

The people who ran Fort Lauderdale were not pleased by Howard's double-barrel assault. This anarchy, they said, would ruin the beach. But Howard did not stop at the beach. Howard played his song again and again, with startling results.

One judge agreed that it was unconstitutional to arrest a woman who cursed at a police officer. Another threw out a state law that allowed police to give alcohol tests to drivers who passed out. A third delivered the biggest shock to Fort Lauderdale's guardians of propriety by striking down the law against public drinking.

Howard asked how the city could arrest homeless people for drinking wine in a park while selling beer at its own festivals in the same park. The city attorney said it was a simple matter of taste.

"People don't like to look at hobos drinking," he said.

The judge sat up.

"Some people don't like to look at sick people, or people in wheel chairs," the judge said. "Shall we arrest them too? Shall we just go ahead and arrest anyone you don't like to look at?"

The city attorney did not answer. Howard won again.

In all, Howard persuaded judges to declare eight Fort Lauderdale laws unconstitutional, and every case brought more newspaper stories, more time on the television news, more interviews. Howard liked being interviewed as much as reporters liked to interview Howard. They liked to interview him because they liked him.

Many of them felt the way Howard did about the war, about the poor, about drugs. Many had protested or picketed or sat in, or wanted to. A lot of them became reporters for the reasons Howard became a lawyer, to change things, and Howard reminded them.

It was easy to forget along the mind-dulling march of city

commission meetings and traffic accidents and weather stories that had become their work lives. The people they covered, the people they listened to and wrote about, were people like their parents, the people who told them to get haircuts and get married and wear ties. Howard was different, and wonderful. Howard was on their side.

Reporters couldn't write fast enough to take down all they wanted, but there was always more. He was a friend, but he was also the uncle who always had something special in his pocket. Reporters quickly learned that whenever they needed a good story, or a good quote about social issues, or even just a good laugh, they could call Howard and he would spin the tale of his latest joust with authority. It wasn't long before Howard became the story. Less than a year out of law school, he was profiled in three newspapers. One of them called him the ponytailed gladiator of civil rights.

Howard liked that. The ponytailed gladiator.

Howard was sure, after that recognition, that he would never cut his hair again. He was more eager to joust than ever. Howard used these stories to open new fronts in his war for the constitution.

"The government has no business legislating morality," he said, over and over, and called for the repeal of laws against prostitution and drug use, including heroin.

Every mesmerized reporter helped Howard drape himself in the thin cloth of a selfless man who cared only for the rights of others, but one spied his gaudier clothes, too.

"It's a show," Howard said. "The criminal defense lawyer is the actor in me. I'll cry for them, and I'll make them cry. I'll make them go through every fact and emotion in the human body, and only then will I rest. If they are going to decide against my client, they are going to feel that they are sentencing themselves too."

There were others at 25 who understood the power of emotion, others who could use it effectively, but not many at any age who could keep from being burned by the heat. For a man who fought so hard and so well, Howard made remarkably few enemies. He tried to cooperate with everyone, even the people he beat in court, and he was always careful when he attacked the law not to attack the people who supported it.

The reporters found out that the people who hated what Howard was doing did not hate Howard.

"He's just doing his job," said the assistant city attorney who faced Howard and lost in case after case.

Howard kept his politeness and good humor despite a draining workload. By summer, Howard had been promoted to the felony division, and he never had less than 50 clients at a time. They were all poor, all desperate. The beachside sleepers and drinkers that won headlines for Howard had little to lose except a few nights in the county jail. The people he represented now faced hard time, and they had little to offer in their own defense except faith, which they did not give easily.

Many had no idea who Howard was, even after he explained, even after the judge explained. He would tell them to tell him everything, to trust him, to let him help. And they would just stare back at his ponytail and ask: "Who are you?"

Howard answered by winning. People on the street who knew nothing about constitutional challenges and newspaper profiles and public defenders heard about Ponytail, the free lawyer who didn't lose. His reputation, on the street and in the courts, grew when he cleared John Charles Gern of murder. Everyone expected him to lose.

Gern, college student and hustler, confessed to shooting the manager of a gay movie house. The state also had a witness, the man Gern was escorting that night. Howard was assigned to the case with his friend and professional opposite, Channing Brackey.

Brackey was smarter than Howard, and probably a better lawyer. He was certainly more scholarly. Howard could not wait to get into a courtroom, to take his turn on stage, but he had no patience for rehearsal. He was no more inclined to scour casebooks for precedents than to cut his hair.

Howard just wanted the chance to persuade a jury. Brackey

didn't believe in taking such chances, perhaps because he wasn't as persuasive. He wouldn't dream of going to court until he had exhausted his law books and himself in search of every angle, every advantage. None had been discovered when it came time to try John Gern.

Gern disowned his halting, muddled confession, but there was no evidence the police beat it out of him. They didn't have to. Gern was so scared, so confused, that by the time police were through questioning him, he was curled in fetal position, chewing the flesh from his arms. He had told them enough to be charged with murder, later reduced to manslaughter. Gern said he found the gun in the theater and wanted to turn it in. He didn't know it was loaded. Instead of handing it to the manager, Robert Meadows, he pulled the trigger.

Gern's lawyers could not get the confession thrown out, and they could not stop the jury from hearing it. They had nothing to contradict the testimony of the witness, a heavy, middle-aged man named Jay Seides who was a regular police informant. It was Seides who turned in Gern after police threatened to consider him a suspect in the killing. Howard listened carefully as Seides testified for the prosecution, but he was more interested in what he saw.

Howard saw Seides' eyes darting back and forth as he spoke. He saw that Seides was breathing heavily, and sweating. Howard saw a man about to burst under pressure. He decided to see how much more he could stand.

When it was his turn to ask questions, Howard started slow and friendly, but Seides was flustered from the start. Howard asked simple questions, but he asked them hard and fast. And he stared right into Seides' eyes, held them in one place so that he couldn't use them to escape.

"You don't know who shot him, do you?"

"No," Seides said.

"You don't even know if you shot him, do you?"

"No," Seides said.

That was all. If there was anyone more flustered than the

witness, it was the prosecutor. When he made his closing remarks, he pointed to the defendant and said: "This man is the killer."

Then he pointed to his own witness and said: "Or he is."

The jury reached its verdict in 14 minutes. The judge was startled by shouts of joy from the gallery.

"Ladies and gentlemen," he shouted, "you are admonished to restrain yourselves."

He was shouting at Howard's family. Howard drew his own admonishment when he slammed his hands against the defense table and jumped in the air.

"Mr. Finkelstein, you certainly know better," the judge said.

At that moment, Howard felt that he knew everything.

The eyes of truth

Howard stuffed a bloody shirt in his mouth, because they were wrong.

Since he started law school, people had been telling him that a real courtroom is not like television. Now he knew the truth. It was like television, but better, because he was the star, and he was getting bigger and brighter with every performance. Howard handled the strangest cases with a captivating strangeness of his own, and it worked.

"All the jurors have seen Perry Mason," he told a reporter. "They want a show, and I love a captive audience."

He loved it enough to make jurors gasp as he bit into a dead man's shirt and screamed. He wanted them to see and hear how the victim died, gagged and screaming, and he wanted them to believe his client was not the killer. The jury believed, and Howard won.

He loved it enough to fling open a sack of sex toys while arguing the case for a pornographer. Howard showered the jury with large, plastic dildos, and they all laughed, especially the old ladies. He won again.

The Howard Show drew the biggest crowds, and the most cameras, at the Broward County Courthouse. Secretaries, clerks, bailiffs, other lawyers, even judges came to see his stunts. Some came to study, and learn. He was the talk of the hallways, and he talked back. Howard had a smile, and a hello by name, for everyone, even the prosecutors. When Howard passed, people nudged each other, as though they had seen someone special, because they had.

Howard loved it, all of it. No matter where he went, to work or to a restaurant or to a party, he was the center of attention. He never stopped to tell himself that he shouldn't let all the praise go to his head. He wanted it there. He wanted a head as big as a head could be, big enough to make a five-foot-three lawyer stand above the crowd. He deserved to feel good about himself because he was still following the good path, the right path, with his eyes closed. He opened them just once, long enough to look into the eyes of Benjamin LeParre, and then he closed them tight.

Benjamin LeParre was 17 and very strong and a long way from his home in New Hampshire when Dr. Wallace Knight, 53, picked him up hitchhiking along Interstate 95 on Aug. 10, 1979. A neighbor heard screams that night and rushed into Knight's apartment with a gun. Knight had been stabbed 14 times. LeParre was standing over him, holding a knife, covered in blood.

The case started as another odd and obvious loser for Finkelstein and Brackey, but this time there was no chance for Howard's theatrics. Dr. Knight died before the trial—of cancer, not his wounds. He left a taped statement, accusing LeParre of robbing and then stabbing him. It was enough to get LeParre indicted as an adult, but not to convict him. The defense team found a technicality in state law that prevented juveniles from being indicted for any crime that did not carry a life sentence. The maximum sentence for attempted murder was 30 years. An appeals court threw out the indictment, and LeParre went free. The newspapers played it up big.

But while they were preparing the case, Howard looked his client in the eye and felt a chill he had never felt as a lawyer. He had always believed his clients were innocent—not that they had a right to be presumed innocent, but that they really were. He believed that even if they did what the prosecutors claimed, there was a reason, a good reason that he could explain to a jury if he could only understand it. Howard looked his clients in the eye and saw the fear, the hurt, the anger, and it helped.

Then he looked into the eyes of Benjamin LeParre, a boy who hacked down every tree in his neighborhood when he was eight years old just because he wanted to. Howard saw nothing: No fear, no hurt, no anger. "This man could kiss me or kill me," Howard thought, "and he would never think twice about either."

These were the coldest, hardest eyes he had ever seen, and Howard was afraid. He wasn't afraid of Benjamin LeParre. He was afraid that if he looked into them again, he couldn't believe any more.

Howard had always been afraid to be wrong, but he was most afraid, deep down, of being wrong about his clients. Howard was not a religious man, but he was a spiritual man, and he believed he had a gift. He believed the force that chose him for this work also chose the people who needed his help, and that they were good people. He did not want to believe it was random, or worse, that he had a choice. Howard never wanted to choose if he could believe instead. He could only work so hard, and so well, if there was no doubt he was doing right. Howard turned away from Benjamin LeParre and closed his eyes again and tried hard never to think about it.

He had plenty of distractions. The star of the courthouse was not only an exciting man to see, he was an exciting man to be seen with. He was invited to dinner or parties all week, every week, and when there was no party, Howard started one.

He loved Kelly, but he began excusing himself from her performances. It's professional, he explained, a way of making contacts. It was also a way of meeting women in black dresses that were slit to the thigh. If college was an amusement park of sex and drugs, the courthouse was Disney World.

Women thought Howard was adorable, and they always wanted to go somewhere to hear more of his stories. Men thought Howard was interesting, too, and funny—and too short to be a threat. Howard was not only invited to more parties packed with lawyers, judges and newspaper reporters, he was invited into the bathrooms. He was invited to share the cocaine.

Howard did not know how dangerous that was, because he

did not see the difference. In college, in the early '70s, drugs bound friends together and welcomed new ones to the circle. Everybody shared, and they shared with open hands. Everyone smoked marijuana and ate LSD and swallowed Quaaludes. In the dorm, they would all sit and smoke and sing and talk, with nothing to hide, not their drugs and not their feelings. The difference between their drugs and cocaine was that they couldn't afford cocaine.

Howard tried it for the first time when his roommate brought some to their room in the Desoto Dorm. He laughed at the idea of putting a straw in his nose. The two of them sucked in all the cocaine, and laughed, and went back to smoking pot. He didn't try it again for a long time, because no one had any, but he thought about it. He thought about how clean it was, how clean it smelled. He thought about the delicious, numbing instant it touched the back of his throat and began to trickle down, like the warm trickle from a dentist's needle. Howard could taste it whenever he thought about it, and when he tasted it, he could feel the flash in his head.

Howard did not try cocaine again for a long time, but he thought about it, and the next time it was offered, he was eager to accept. He did not realize for years how eager he was, until he remembered what happened in law school. Howard was studying for exams and he bought some amphetamine pills that would keep him awake and alert through the long night of cramming. But he didn't swallow them. He crushed the pills and inhaled them, as though they were cocaine.

Long before Howard understood the power of cocaine, he felt the power of its ritual. The people who invited him into the bathrooms at parties understood both. Alone or in very small groups, they laid out their razors and straws as a priest lays out his chalice and cross, and they gloried in themselves. It was no accident that they lined their powder on mirrors, where they could see themselves, or that they closed the door, so others couldn't see them. They were not trying to keep a secret, not the way they talked or dressed or walked away with white-tipped noses. They wanted others to feel left out, the ones who did not deserve to join them, the ones who were not as brave and smart and successful.

When they invited Howard to join them in the bathroom, he thought they were being friendly and generous and polite, like a college kid offering to share a joint, like a neighbor offering a cup of coffee. They weren't. They were trying to buy his glory, to bathe themselves in the star's reflection. They were trying to make him one of them, so they could be like him.

It is hard today for Howard to look back and believe that he did not sense it, that he was not repelled by the hypocrisy. These people weren't hippies who hoped and believed, right or wrong, that their drugs held answers. These people didn't want answers and they asked no questions. The money, and the times, were too good to be spoiled. The profits of war were too great.

The children of Howard's children will study these times and that war someday, but Howard was there, almost from the beginning. When he was in high school, Howard never thought much about where marijuana came from or why. He thought it should be legal, of course, and free. That's why, when he was young, Howard had no use for smugglers and dealers, not because they broke the law but because they made money from something Howard thought everyone should share.

To Howard, selling drugs would be like selling the ocean, but that was certainly not unthinkable in South Florida. Howard had come to live in a place where, legal or not, it was fair game to make money on everything, no matter how dumb or dangerous. Millions came for the beach, but developers built a wall of condominiums so no one could see it. Politicians took money to let the developers do it, and inspectors took money to let them do it badly. Howard the socialist had come to live in the freest of free markets, and the market for drugs was booming.

The boats came every night from the islands and from South America to dark coves in the Keys and backyard docks in Fort Lauderdale—slow, short boats and fast, long boats and boats so big they were really ships. And everyone saw them, weighted down with dope, struggling along like so many fat men in inner tubes. They might as well have carried billboards, but it wouldn't matter. Who were they hiding from?

They were not hiding from Howard or his friends or their parents, or anyone like them. Marijuana did not jump off those boats. It was unloaded by people who had day jobs at grocery stores and restaurants and police stations. It was driven away in trucks that also carried flowers and doughnuts and toilet paper. It was sold by high school kids and their fathers and their mothers to other high school kids and their fathers and their mothers.

There was a man known as Little Ray Thompson, a man as short as Howard Finkelstein, who sold and smuggled as much marijuana as anyone and only killed a few other men. He bought a marina, a big one, and a fleet of boats, and he hired people to sit on his boats all day, fishing and smiling and waving to everyone who passed. He hired grandmothers. Little Ray Thompson sent his thugs to condominiums to offer money to little old ladies to sit on boats, and none of them asked why, because they didn't have to ask. They took the money.

A lot of people took the money, and a lot of people spent it. It was bad politics to say too much about this, one way or the other. There were hard times in other places, where people worked in factories, but not in South Florida, where so many people didn't work at all, where so many people could make money from drugs without selling them. They only had to put out their hands and take the cash, for diamond rings and teak-decked yachts and drop-top Ferraris. It was a fortune no one could argue with, until cocaine, until the murders.

At first, in the late '70s, it was all in Miami, the papers said. It was all Cubans, or Colombians, or whoever. They carried machine guns, and they fired them. Sometimes they hit each other, and sometimes they hit children. Sometimes their houses blew up. The ether did that, the ether they used to make cocaine. People got scared, especially when the killings spread. It wasn't just Miami, and it wasn't just Cubans or Colombians or whoever. Crazy men were firing machine guns and blowing up houses, and killing cops, all over South Florida, even in Hollywood. People got scared, and so did the politicians. They started talking about a war on drugs, as though a war hadn't already begun. They ordered the police to do something, and the police did. They filled the jails and courts with people whose pockets were filled with enough cash to buy the best lawyers, if not the best judges.

Win or lose in court, the lawyers won at the bank. They worked for cash, sometimes enough from one case to buy a two-seat Mercedes, sometimes enough to buy a house, and perhaps a small bonus in the form of white powder. These were the people Howard was getting to know, the men with the women in black dresses who were known as coke whores. When he thought about it at all, Howard did not think they were bad people, any of them. He had no problem defending a drug dealer, because he believed all drugs should be legal. He used to think it was wrong for lawyers to take money from anyone, because justice should be free for all, but the exhaustion of two years in the public defender's office made him less quick to judge. He was tired and overworked and he could only pretend for so long that he had never looked in Benjamin LeParre's eyes. He did not turn away when they invited him into the bathroom.

Why should he? Who better to glory in himself than the ponytailed gladiator? Cocaine made him feel even stronger, even braver. It also made him feel more like the people around him and less like the hippie who thought it was wrong to take money for helping someone. Howard was the star of the courthouse, and he made $32,000 a year. Men who made 10 times that much were giving him cocaine and asking him for free advice. Howard started to wonder what it would be like to be one of them, even while telling himself he never would be. He started to stay out all night.

Kelly was patient, for a long time, with Howard's ego and Howard's drugs. Her friends were no angels either. The musicians that Howard met through Kelly would have snorted as much cocaine as the lawyers, if they had the money. They bought what they could, and Howard joined them when he came to see Kelly. It wasn't just the drugs that chased her away. She knew Howard was changing, and Kelly was changing too. The more Howard dreamed about the things a successful lawyer could have, the boats and cars and suits, the more Kelly dreamed about a world where none of that mattered. As Howard turned away from the '60s, Kelly threw herself back toward them. She began to see a mystic who told her to give up worldy goods and worldly men. He told her to leave Howard.

When Howard came home, late and high, as he did in high school, he argued with Kelly, as he had argued with his mother. He went to work tired and depressed, before his day even began. For every big case that won him headlines, Howard struggled to carry 50 that no one noticed. They dragged on and on and dragged him down. All day, every day, he shuttled from cellblock to courtroom, trying to help people who could not help themselves. He had begun to see the same faces a second time, and a third. He answered the same questions again and again.

Howard did not want to look in their eyes anymore. In the fall of 1980, at 27, Howard was losing the path and he was starting to panic.

For anyone else, the solution would be simple and obvious. No one stays in the public defender's office more than a few years, unless he wants to be an administrator. The other young defenders who started when Howard did were nearly all gone, to the prosecutor's office, where there were political connections to be made, or to private practice, where there was money. For a long time, Howard didn't want to think about any of it. He had no use for bosses, so he could never be an administrator. He could never be a prosecutor, because he would lose all his reasons for being a lawyer. And he did not want to believe he could do anything just for money, even as he dreamed about the boats and cars and women. For Howard, the doors that everyone else escaped through were closed, at least in his mind. So he kept his eyes closed as long and as tight as he could and he felt the pressure rise as he ran as fast as he could, until he ran into Robert Sherwood.

When he came back from Vietnam, Sherwood had no notion of how to make a living except by using the power of his fists. He liked to hurt people, and learned quickly to find people who wanted to be hurt. Masochists, men who were thrilled by pain, paid Sherwood to beat them up. The manager of the Photo-Finish Lounge across from Gulfstream racetrack, paid Sherwood $200 to give him a rough time. Sherwood tied him to a chair, gagged him, and beat his face until it bled. The manager never got out of the chair. He was found there the next morning, dead and disfigured. The cash register, and his pockets, were empty.

Sherwood wasn't hard to find. He talked too much about his work, and the people he talked to told the police. Sherwood confessed to the beating, but he swore that the bar manager was still alive when he left. Police charged him with murder.

Howard defended his client with honest passion. He attacked a war that turned decent men into killers and a government that rewarded them for abandoning all sense of decency. He argued that Sherwood suffered delayed stress from combat, nerve damage from the chemicals used to destroy the jungles, and self-hatred from all the killing. If Robert Sherwood was a degraded man who degraded others, he was still a victim.

But Howard's impassioned argument wasn't enough to save Sherwood, and he knew it. He could not prove that Sherwood left the victim alive, but he didn't have to. Howard merely had to raise a doubt, reasonable though small, that he committed murder. This was the great irony of Howard's life as a lawyer: the man who rushed through life with his eyes closed, believing without question that he was following the right path, had a great and natural talent for raising doubt in others. This is the simple beauty of criminal law, the reason Howard could scribble through his legal homework and still win in court: The defense doesn't have to prove a thing. In the case of Robert Sherwood, Howard did not have to prove the gypsies did it. He simply suggested they could have, if they were there at all.

It was the carnival that gave him the idea. The racetrack

was closed for the season, but the grounds were taken over by the annual county fair. Along with the cows and cowboys and pie-eating contests came the carnival rides and the carnival games and the carnival men wearing the dirt of a thousand small towns. Sherwood said he saw them when he left the bar, and they asked him if it was open. Howard asked the jury this: "How do you know those men didn't go into the bar and find the manager all tied up and decide to finish him off and steal the money? Why would you condemn this brave man who fought for his country before you would suspect those cons and thugs who cheat children out of quarters?"

It was a good question, Howard thought, maybe good enough to save his client, but he couldn't be sure. He needed the final dramatic touch that would sweep the jurors into his corner. He held his breath until it was very near the end, and the table remained for the taking.

Neither side had made much of it during the trial, except to note that it existed: a three-legged, dusty rattan table with a handprint on top, a hand printed in human blood. It wasn't the victim's hand, and it wasn't Robert Sherwood's hand. Howard held his breath all trial long, expecting the prosecutor to defuse this powerful weapon for the defense. The print could have belonged to an accomplice, to one of the carnies, to a cop. The print didn't prove a thing, but Howard didn't have to. When it was time for his closing argument, Howard carried the table into the courtroom, hoisted it into the jury box and pointed to the blood.

"This is the killer's hand!" Howard shouted. "This is the man who should be convicted!"

The jury let Robert Sherwood go free.

Howard accepted the usual congratulations, and congratulated himself. He felt good about this fight, better than most lately, because it wasn't all show. He had raised serious issues, about the war and the way America treated the men who fought it, and he had learned something important about the way he had passed judgment on those men. It was a case that made him want to go on and forget all the pressure and doubts.

He was excited, again, and eager when Al Schreiber sent him to Las Vegas for a series of legal seminars with other public defenders from across the country. He stepped up front for a group photo, smiling up at the tall, beautiful photographer who might have been one of the hotel's showgirls. She looked back through her lens and screamed.

"Howie! Howie Finkelstein!"

Howard had no idea who she was.

"It's Donna, from school. Donna Chase."

Howard had only the vaguest memory of the woman who surprised him by repeating so much of what he'd said in political science class. He was even more surprised that she knew about his work. For years, a friend had been sending Donna newspaper stories about the man who won her admiration and anger in college, but he had forgotten her. He had forgotten, but he wasn't blind. He took her phone number back to Florida and promised to stay in touch.

When he got back home, Howard was relaxed and revitalized, certain that he was in the right place doing the right job. Then he got a call from Robert Sherwood.

His former client was in Pennsylvania, and he wanted Howard to fly there, right away, to be his lawyer. Sherwood had been charged with murdering two more customers.

Howard felt sick and scared at the same time. Now he could never forget the look in Benjamin LeParre's eyes. Now the doubts were all his.

Into the '80s, alone

Howard quit his job.

In January of 1981, Howard went to his boss, Al Schreiber, and thanked him for everything. Then he cleaned out his desk and files and drove seven blocks to a small house at 1310 SW 3rd Avenue.

The neighborhood around the courthouse was filled with houses like this, old stucco houses with wood floors and tile roofs. Nobody wanted these houses anymore except the lawyers. One by one, the houses near the river became offices and some became beautiful. The big firms laid down hard tile and hung thick doors of oak and brass. Howard and his new partner, Channing Brackey, who had also quit the public defender's office, settled for fresh paint, beige throughout.

Now Howard could not be trapped and fooled by chance. He did not have to look Benjamin LeParre in the eye or take calls from Robert Sherwood. He did not even have to take money, except from people who could afford to pay him, but the money, he believed, would come. Everyone said so. Everyone would want the ponytailed gladiator. He didn't even have to advertise.

Defender hangs it up to hang own shingle,

read the headline on yet another newspaper profile depicting Howard as a brilliant and courageous man who promised to fight for the poor and helpless.

Kelly tried to tell him that going into private practice

wouldn't make him happy. But Howard was tired of hearing her lectures and tired of making excuses to get away. He told her just that. He told her he liked his new, powerful friends, and the women in black-slit dresses. He hurt her, and he chased her away.

Howard came home one day, soon after moving into his new office, and saw Kelly with her bags packed. She wished him the best and left to live in a commune in California. She left with another man, and Howard could not believe who it was. Kelly left to live in a commune with the son of Ed Stack, the sheriff.

Of all the rude shocks the real world had given him, this was the worst, the one that chased Howard away as surely as he had chased Kelly. How could this happen, now? Howard had made himself taller than ever to everyone else, but the woman he loved made him small again. He was never so angry, or so scared. He never felt such a need to escape.

For a long time, it was enough to know that he could go when he needed, once or twice a week, to his second world—to cocaine. Now he wanted to be there whenever he couldn't be in a courtroom. Whatever haunted Howard stayed outside the courtroom, panting beside the wide, brown doors. Inside, Howard ruled.

Inside, his clients were always innocent, always good, and Howard was always right. Whatever followed Howard when he walked out those doors, whatever howled and bared its teeth at night, could be tamed again in an instant, in one sharp breath of cocaine.

Howard still smoked grass every day, but that was different. He would dig his hands deep into the moist, earthy ball and roll a joint without really thinking about it. He smoked it while he read books or watched television or talked on the phone, letting its sweet heat soak slowly into his lungs. It might make him smile at his demons, but it did not chase them away.

Cocaine chased everything away. Cocaine was a demanding, jealous bitch and Howard was already too deep in love to argue. Cocaine was too good to be touched. Howard was hypnotized by the bright, sterile whiteness, and his heart pumped hard as he chopped it into fine powder. He trembled each time he lifted the silver straw to his nose and took his first, sharp breath. If it took any time at all for the cocaine to reach his brain, it was the time it takes lightning to burst across the sky and slap the earth. Cocaine was lightning, and Howard felt it explode. But the light stayed, a light brighter and hotter and clearer than any light in the real world. With the light of cocaine in his eyes, Howard could see anything but demons and he could do anything he wanted.

Who would not breathe deep?

So many others tried and suffocated. Howard could not miss seeing them, because he was so close. He saw them in courtrooms and jail cells, and in the morgue. But they held no lesson, because Howard was too smart. He was smart enough to know that cocaine was not addictive, smart enough to keep his pleasures in their proper place, smart enough to know when he'd had enough, smart enough to keep his worlds from colliding.

Of all the lessons Howard finally learned, this hurt the most: Howard isn't as smart as he thought he was.

But he was smart enough to sense one defect in the power of cocaine, and to step back just enough to avoid a terrible fall. When he was high, he couldn't talk right. No matter how brilliant his thoughts, he could not get them past his teeth. Even the next day, his tongue tripped over every other word.

The one time he went to court high, he was embarrassed. Worse, he couldn't do his job, not as well as Howard needed to do his job. That's when he knew, for sure, that he had to keep his worlds apart. He still believed he could. Howard loved being a lawyer, and he loved cocaine. He was thankful that he didn't have to choose. There would simply be no cocaine in the office.

That did not mean there would be no drugs. Every afternoon, when Howard was certain he'd had his last hearing of the day, he would swing his feet up on top of his huge, teak desk and light a joint. This was the best thing about private practice. He could lean back and smoke a joint right in the office and no one would say a word. He would have been shocked if anyone did. After all, he never tried to hide. In all those newspaper profiles, Howard always worked in a plea for legalizing drugs. His views were so well known that reporters called him for quotes whenever the subject was raised. It was the same with prostitution. Howard took every opportunity to argue that it should be legalized.

Like the drug boats clogging the marinas, he might as well have held up a sign: "I take drugs and I share them with women in black-slit dresses who will do anything for cocaine." Even if he did, he was certain, no one would say a thing.

Despite his doubts and demons, Howard still had the charm and humor and decency that kept him from making enemies while winning cases. He still had the powerful will to be liked, and he made the most unlikely allies. That single time Howard went to court high on cocaine, the judge motioned him toward the bench, flicked a finger back and forth across her own nose and winked. Howard winked back, and wiped the white powder away.

When a policeman stopped him for driving crazy and handcuffed him behind his back, the chief came along and winked, just like the judge. The policeman let Howard go and called him a cab. Everyone understood that Howard was different, especially his clients.

Howard began a private practice that rivaled his experience in the public defender's office for strange cases and publicity. When a disgruntled police officer was charged with firing bullets at his chief's house, he hired Howard the hippie to defend him. When that same chief was about to be fired a few weeks later, he hired Howard to fight city hall. Howard won both cases.

A computer analyst hired Howard to save him from 31 years in prison. The man was drunk when he drove off the road and killed two elderly motorcycle riders parked along the side. He left them there and drove away, but a police officer caught him, tested him for alcohol, and locked him up. Even Howard could not make a jury doubt what happened, but he didn't have to. He looked the judge straight in the eye and said it didn't matter. His client suffered from a rare sleeping sickness that took control of his mind without warning, he said. Drunk or not, he would have crashed in the same place, with the same results. He could not be held responsible.

The prosecutor gave up. He said Howard would only confuse the jury, and he offered a deal. Instead of going to jail for 31 years, Howard's client went to jail for 45 days, and he went home every night.

Howard was good at negotiating pleas, a valuable skill when most cases never get to trial because there aren't enough judges or courtrooms or jail cells. Howard was good because he was the other side's best incentive to avoid a jury. And he was good because he was realistic. He understood that the other side needed to save face. He never tried to embarrass or belittle anyone, not the prosecutor; not the judge.

That is one way the real courtroom was different from television. There was no feud between the defense lawyers and the prosecutors, nothing personal for most, win or lose. Howard was glad about that, because he wanted so much to be liked. But it also bothered him that lawyers could so neatly separate themselves from their fights when their fights were about other people's lives. It bothered him that no one in the courtroom was really interested in the truth—not the judge, who wanted to go home on time, and not the prosecutor, who wanted everyone to go to jail, and not Howard, who could not let himself believe he was wrong.

What bothered him most was how he changed.

The young Howard who shouted for student rights at high school rallies would never sit down afterward to have coffee and tell jokes with the principal. Howard the lawyer who shouted for his clients' rights in court could joke and shake hands and play tennis and slap the backs of men who would send his clients to prison. Howard learned to do business that way, and he was learning, painfully, that law was a business.

For the first time, Howard had to worry about paying the rent, paying his secretary and holding up his end of a partnership. For the first time, Howard had to talk to his clients about money. At first, he didn't know how to do it, and he never learned to do it well. He never got over the feeling that it was dirty talk.

As a public defender, Howard never had to think about the cost of fighting a case instead of pleading guilty, or of flying in an expert witness or of ordering his own tests on a weapon or corpse. Now, he had to ask the people who wanted his help how much justice they could afford, and he had to tell them when it wasn't enough. He hated that. He would not go back on his promise to help the poor, and Howard worked often for as little as he could. As surely as word spread that Howard was a good lawyer, word spread that he was a soft touch.

At a time when the big names charged $50,000 for the average drug trafficking case, Howard charged $7,500, maybe $10,000 if the client could afford it, and a lot less if the client couldn't. He was an even softer touch at the end of the month, when the bills were due and he had to get on the phone and call clients who were late paying and listen to their sad stories. Howard needed to make $13,000 every month just to pay the bills. If it wasn't there, he needed to drum up as much business as he could. At the end of some months, he would take a case for $750.

Howard knew people were taking advantage of him, but for all his ego, he found it hard to say: "I'm sorry, but you can't afford me." He knew a lot of lawyers who said it every day and some who used their clients' fear to take more than their share. He knew lawyers who spent as much time studying their clients' bank accounts as they did preparing a case. He knew one lawyer who waited until the first day of a trial, when his client was most vulnerable, and put his hand out, like a bellhop, before he would walk into court.

No matter how much he needed money, Howard would never put his hand out, and he never had to. Howard's reputation grew. For every client who wanted something for nothing, there were plenty of others eager to pay cash for Howard's help. Nearly all of them were accused of selling drugs. Even when Howard charged $10,000, he was more than a bargain.

Eventually, Howard was representing celebrity-class drugsters like Little Ray Thompson, the man with the flotilla of grandmothers. Drug dealers brought Howard cash in bags and bundles and shoe boxes and dumped it on his desk, because that is how the criminal law business worked. It's one thing to believe a client is honest but quite another to take his personal check.

The first time a client dumped cash on his desk, Howard could not stop staring. A man who robbed restaurants brought Howard a box filled with $3,500 in fives and ones. Howard stared and wondered: "Why would anyone bring me all this when I'd represent him for nothing?"

But Howard did not turn the cash away. Howard put away enough to pay his bills and his taxes and he put the rest in his pocket. From the time he went into private practice, Howard always had cash in his pocket and that was enough to satisfy him. He still rented the house from his father. He still wore T-shirts and jeans, except when he was in court. Even when he wore a suit, he never spent much because he bought his suits in the boys' department.

The only sign of success that Howard wore were his boots. Howard had been wearing boots since high school, thick-soled leather. Now he wore snakeskin boots, hand-tooled, $175 a pair. He had long since given up the orange VW van for a Pontiac Grand Prix, but now he traded the Pontiac for a sports car, a black 280Z. Still, the cars and a few pairs of boots did not empty his pockets. He always had a few hundred dollars ready to buy drinks for his friends at the bars on Las Olas Boulevard. He always had money for cocaine. Howard spent the cash as fast as he made it, and he has never been sure where it went. He got rid of it quickly because he felt guilty about taking it.

Howard liked to tell the joke about the woman who called a plumber because her sink was clogged. The plumber hit the drain pipe with a wrench and the water ran out. He handed her a bill for $200. For hitting the wrench with a pipe? "No," he said, "for knowing where to hit it." That's why people dumped money on Howard's desk—because he knew where to bang the legal pipes—and he thought that was wrong. He thought the justice system in America should be good enough and decent enough and fair enough to run free and strong for everyone, not just the ones who could afford a lawyer who knew where to bang the pipes. He still thought so, even after he knew it would never be, even after he started to take the money.

Howard was surely wrong about one or the other, about the system or about taking the money, but he wasn't greedy. If Howard were greedy, he could have been rich.

The money some of his clients dumped on his desk meant nothing to them except the price of doing business. Their real money was in the boats and bales and kilos of their trade, in the gold around their necks, in their homes on the water. Howard knew that other lawyers, a few at least, found a way to share the wealth. No matter what they charged for their services, they could make far more as partners in the drug trade and they could keep their hands clean. It was a simple matter of introducing a 10 o'clock appointment to an 11 o'clock appointment, or of passing along a name or a number. They were brokers, agents, coordinators, not gangsters. They were greedy, and Howard wasn't. If he broke the law, and he did, it was for pleasure, never for gain.

He never took drugs from his clients as payment. He did not want to do anything that could cost him his license.

But he did take drugs from his clients, the ones he called friends, as gifts. Howard got to know the top dealers and their distributors, and he liked a lot of them. He even dated one for a while, a cocaine dealer named Linda. Whatever their image anywhere else, drug dealers were the high social caste of criminal clients. Many belonged to yacht clubs, and many went to college. Howard found them easier to talk to than burglars, and they liked the idea of a good lawyer who worked cheap.

They liked to show him off, and Howard liked that. Howard was still pretty then, before the cocaine started to rot his teeth and sear his skin. The drug dealers dressed him up and showed off their ponytailed lawyer, the way they showed off the women in black-slit dresses.

Howard got closer to these people than he ever expected, close enough to feel their fear and to share it. For all their show and all their wealth and all their talk, there was no real joy among them. For all the thrill of cocaine, it did not make anyone Howard ever met happy.

He never saw anyone smiling on the way to the bathroom, or on the way out.

Even standing at parties, they pulled their arms in tight, hugging their cocaine and their chains and their silk suits as though they were afraid it would all disappear, because it could. Even when they felt safe from the government, they could not feel safe from each other.

Howard could defend them in court, but he could not defend them on the street or in their homes or in their Ferraris. He could not stop bullets. At first, and for a long time, Howard did not think about that. He knew that his clients took professional risks, but he did not see what that had to do with him, until he met Roger Stark.

The very first time they met, Roger told him to be careful.

Careful? Howard thought that was odd advice. "Why should I be careful?"

"Because," Roger said, "someone is going to kill you."

Howard did not believe Roger, but he did not ignore him. He knew too many other people who were worried about being killed, with good reason. So Howard laughed, but he did not walk away.

"Just for the sake of argument," Howard asked, "why would anyone want to kill me?"

"Because of Linda," Roger said. "Your former girlfriend is an informant. Linda is helping the police make a case against Barry Hunwick."

Barry Hunwick. Howard heard that name, and he started to feel the fear. That was the name the drug dealers all knew, and all worried about, before any of it made the papers. They all said Barry Hunwick would kill anyone for money, and that other dealers hired him to kill their rivals.

Howard began to feel the fear, but he pushed it away, even

when Roger said Hunwick wanted him dead because he thought Linda had told him too much.

"I'm just a lawyer," Howard said. "No one kills lawyers."

Howard did not believe any of it, because he did not want to believe any of it, until asked Linda: You don't happen to know a guy named Barry Hunwick, do you?

"I know him," she said, "and I told the police all about him."

A few nights later, as Howard was driving home, he heard a shot. He did not see the other car until it raced away, but he heard the shot he heard his tire explode and he felt his car jerk away from him. He pulled hard on the wheel and ran off the road.

It could have been a mistake, and Howard knew that. In South Florida in the 1980s, shooting at other cars was virtually a popular sport. The gunman might have confused Howard with some other asshole who cut him off or flipped him the bird or just looked at him funny. But Howard could not believe that, because he was too close to the people who lived in fear.

When he got home, he called Roger and asked him to help.

It is easy for Howard to see now that this is what Roger wanted, so easy that it is hard to believe he fell for it. But Howard fell as hard as Howard has ever fallen. Nothing that Andy taught him, nothing he read in Marx or Cleaver, nothing he learned in political science class or law school had prepared him to deal with men who killed other men for money.

Howard may have learned where to bang the legal pipes, but he did not really understand where the sludge flowed, or how. It was easy to act tough in court, where he was only acting, but this was different. The lawyers who made $50,000 or $100,000 or $250,000 for defending these men knew something more than law. They knew about evil, and Howard didn't. Howard asked Roger to teach him.

Howard the lawyer listened to Roger's stories about drug wars the way a child listens to ghost stories, and he believed.

"If Hunwick goes down, there is going to be blood in the streets," Roger said. "And it is going to be your blood."

Howard asked him: "What can I do?"

"Trust me," Roger said. "Just trust me".

Howard did, and he was certain it was right. Roger moved into Howard's house, where he could be close, and he went along to bars and parties. They shared women and they shared drugs and Howard felt safe. Roger was not only bigger, he was tougher, and he talked tougher. He always carried a gun.

Howard hated guns, but knew that they were all around. In South Florida, it seemed, everyone had a gun, especially the people Howard spent his time with. Roger promised Howard that nothing would happen as long as he was around.

Even though he trusted Roger, Howard never stopped worrying that something would happen. He had never heard of cocaine-induced paranoia, but he was beginning to live it.

Less than a year after he opened his practice, Howard was breaking the law every day, buying and using a drug that men died for. He was starting to worry about being caught, and to worry that he would have to stop. He worried that cocaine wouldn't help him any more. The magic powder that made demons disappear was losing its magic. It took more and more to set off the lightning that Howard needed.

He did not stop worrying until the night they met Jeff, and then he worried about nothing at all for three days. Jeff taught Howard about freebase.

Jeff worked for one of the biggest smuggling operations in South Florida. He wasn't yet 30 years old, but he owned a chalet on Lake Tahoe and a $1 million seaside home. He was a generous host. When a friend invited Howard to a party at Jeff's house, Howard was also invited to share a powerful new ritual: heating cocaine with a flame and mixing it with ether.

The effect was profound. If cocaine held the power of lightning, freebase cocaine held the power of the atom. Instead of breathing powder, Howard breathed the burning, etherized essence of madness. The demons vanished in a fireball. He sat up with his new friend for three days, smoking freebase all the time.

After that, Howard and Roger spent many hours, many days, exploring the freebase universe together. Roger did not have to worry about going to work. If he had business to conduct, and he did, he could conduct it in Howard's house—in their house. People came and gave him money, and he gave them cocaine.

Howard didn't see this, and Howard didn't want to see this any more than Roger wanted a witness. But Howard saw the money and Howard saw the cocaine, and Howard is not stupid. One time, a man who worked for a big tool company couldn't pay Roger, so Roger took his truck away. Roger took the man's truck and parked it on Howard's lawn. Howard did not ask why.

There was only one time that Howard saw a lot of cocaine, maybe a pound, maybe two. A little cocaine was dangerous enough, but that much could mean a trafficking conviction.

"Get that out of my house," Howard shouted, and Roger did.

Howard did not want to go to jail, and he did not want to lose his license, but he also did not want to be killed by Barry Hunwick, so he could not throw Roger out. When he calmed down, he asked Roger to be careful, and Roger said he would.

"If I see you commit a crime, I can't be your lawyer," Howard said. Roger promised that Howard would never see a thing. The next day, Roger brought home a steel safe and he put a dead-bolt lock on his bedroom door.

Roger asked Howard to rent him the garage, and Howard did, for about what he spent on cigarettes. Howard drew up a lease that said Roger had complete control of the bedroom and the garage, and Roger signed it. He dragged the safe into the garage and locked the door, but whenever Roger opened the door, Howard saw what he kept inside. The garage was filled with television sets and stereos that Roger took in trade.

Howard told himself that they all belonged to the people who brought them. Howard told himself that Roger would not fill his garage with stolen television sets.

Howard told himself whatever he needed to hear to believe that Roger was his friend. Roger protected him, and Roger shared his cocaine. That was enough. If Howard could think about anything except cocaine, he would have seen the terrible mistake, but Howard was certain he could not make mistakes.

He was certain, even as the nose of his 280Z suddenly tilted skyward at 70 or 80 or 90 miles an hour as he was driving home. He was certain, even as the steel below him ripped across the curb and roared. He was certain, even as the car opened itself against the tree and spilled him, like an egg yolk, onto Federal Highway. Howard was certain, and he did not break.

The police did not expect to find anyone alive, but they found Howard. They saw who it was and they laughed. They laughed at the man cocaine had turned to rubber. They laughed and told him to get lost, and Howard was more certain than ever.

Howard went home happy.

He had all the money he needed, a powerful friend to protect him, and a powerful new drug to hide him from all the demons. He had the power to break the law, and the power to break a car without getting hurt. He had the power to buy another one just by signing his name. Howard bought another 280Z, a burgundy coupe with a burgundy interior, and he pasted on a one-word bumper sticker: RADICAL.

Howard could not see anything wrong with his world, not even when Roger started filling his drawers with bullets or bolting gun mounts to the windowsills.

Howard could not see anything wrong, because he could not see anything at all.

A leader lost

Everyone at the courthouse saw him stumbling along, looking like an old man who slept in his clothes when he slept at all, sniffling and snorting and twitching like an old man with an awful cold. But no one thought he had a cold. Everyone knew what had happened to the radical lawyer who made such a big name for himself in such a short time.

Everyone knew Andy Mavrides was a drug addict.

Howard's teacher preceded him in all things: in knowledge, in celebrity, in paranoia and in self-destruction. Howard never stopped adoring him as he followed every step.

When Andy got his law degree, it was as though he shouted for the stage lights to come on, and they did. He ran for the county school board in 1974, and the reporters were as enchanted by his words and ideas as his students had been. Andy won, and he was elected chairman. For three years, the papers were full of Andy's proposals: better schools for blacks, a student seat on the board, a requirement for principals to return to the classroom. Most were rejected by his colleagues, but Andy did not mind losing because it was the fight that mattered. The icon ever-present on the desks of Andy Mavrides was Don Quixote.

The one painful surprise for Andy was the discovery that he couldn't be a lawyer and a politician and be successful at both. He talked about running for the state senate, but he made the harder choice. Three years after entering politics, he quit and decided to work full-time at the law. That did not mean he dedicated himself.

He came to the office late, left early and spent most of the day talking about the great things he would accomplish. Like Howard, Andy was most comfortable talking, not writing briefs or searching through law books. Like Howard, he did not start out looking for money. Andy was always eager to help a friend, or to make a new one. He worked for anyone with a good cause, especially if it was newsworthy. He defended the city's youngest car thief, and its most notorious hit man. But he wanted to use the law for social change and the took company with others who were making it work, black lawyers like Alcee Hastings, who later became a federal judge, who much later was accused of taking bribes and hired Andy Mavrides to defend him. Howard tagged along, and listened, and believed. He knew that if he followed Andy, he followed the path.

He knew Andy was right about the jail. The old cells in the courthouse in downtown Fort Lauderdale were built in the 1920s, and they were dirty and rusty and no bigger than they had to be to hold the handful of drunks and hobos rousted from the gutters of a quiet beach town on Saturday night and released the next morning. Despite additions over the years, there was no fit room for all the men and women of the modern world who were locked away for months while they waited in line for a free courtroom and judge, men and women who were presumed innocent. There was no fit room, but that made no difference. Mattresses were pressed in tight across the floors and bunks stacked to the ceilings. The place stank like an animal pit, because it was.

Andy gagged when he went in there to see clients, and he listened when they asked for his help. He sued the county in federal court, arguing that a jail so crowded was unconstitutional. Years later, when it came time to argue about fees, there were people who said that other lawyers did all the work on the case and that Andy didn't do much except talk. But it was Andy's talk that brought all the stories and pictures and editorials, and kept the case alive in the papers when it might have sat dead in a courthouse file.

It was Andy, impassioned and unyielding, who stood up to

the commissioners and the sheriff and the county judges and demanded, in the name of decency, that they stop. They did, because Andy beat them. A federal judge eventually ordered the county to close the place down and build a new jail. Even then, Andy's suit stayed in force; for years, the county remained under federal order not to jail more people than it had room for and to treat its inmates with care.

At the worst, the inmates were treated better than Andy treated himself. At the worst, they were treated better than a lot of people who trusted Andy Mavrides.

By the time Howard followed him into private practice, Andy had already begun to turn his friends into enemies. Clients complained that he took their cases and their money but did nothing. Some felt cheated, others felt worse. They felt betrayed. The Greeks could not believe that one of their own, son of an immigrant, son of their theater, could do this to them.

The friends who remained friends believed it, because they saw it, but they excused Andy for the same reason people excused Howard: He was so likable. If Andy talked better than he worked, that was no crime. If Andy tried to help people and couldn't, he should be applauded for his instincts, not indicted for his failure. Andy had a good heart, they knew, even when it failed him. It broke down and nearly killed him in 1982, when he was down and being kicked from all sides. He found out his wife was suing him for divorce while he was in the hospital.

If Andy's troubles showed in his shuffling gait and gaunt look, they did not affect his voice. When he was on his feet again, he was full of the old talk and the old charm. He walked into a jewelry store with a woman who looked like a Playboy bunny, and was. Andy called out to the owner in Greek and told him to spread out his gold bracelets. The bunny pointed to one studded with diamonds, and Andy reached into his breast pocket.

Then he sighed. He had forgotten his wallet, he said. The owner shook his head. Andy already owed him $5,000. With this bracelet, it would be $8,000. He always paid Andy's law bills, when Andy did nothing, but when would Andy pay for all the jewelry? Andy smiled and made a promise: He would be back the very next day, with all the money. The jeweler let him have the bracelet, but he was not surprised the next day when Andy did not come. All the jeweler had to show for his trust was a stack of bills signed by Andy Mavrides, in Greek. This time, he hired a different lawyer, and he wasn't alone.

Howard could not believe what he read about his teacher in the paper, and it was all in the paper: the sniffling and the shuffling, the Playboy bunny and the angry jeweler. It was all in the paper after Andy Mavrides disappeared.

The banks and clients were suing him for $250,000, a judge ordered him arrested for contempt, and Andy just ran away to hide.

This time, Howard couldn't follow Andy, no matter how much he wanted to.

Fire in the night

Howard woke up and screamed.

An explosion shattered the wall above his bed, showering him with plaster and old paint, but Howard did not see the wall. He jumped up and screamed and opened his eyes to see the back of a man who was walking calmly out of his bedroom, swinging a shotgun.

Howard screamed for Roger.

The demons that were haunting Howard now did not hide in the creases of his mind. They did not hide at all, and Howard could not hide at all. After the man with the shotgun came into his bedroom, he could not pull the covers over his head and believe they would disappear.

These demons with guns chased him night and day, ever since his car was run off the road. He could not believe these were accidents, or mistakes—not after the firebombs.

Howard was sitting in a soft-back chair smoking cocaine when the first bottle of gasoline crashed through the jalousie windows. He watched it arc across the living room and erupt in the middle of the floor. He watched the orange ball quiver and grow, but he was too high to understand. Was it a pet? By the time Howard realized the fire was not part of his cocaine dream, the second bottle crashed through. Howard stumbled toward the heat and started throwing down everything he could find to smother the flames.

He threw pillows from the couch and dirty clothes that were lying in piles. He stumbled back to the kitchen to get water, and he threw it from glasses as a third bottle exploded.

Howard does not know how many firebombs went off, but there were more, and Howard could not run from one to the next fast enough.

He screamed for Roger, and Roger came. Howard does not know if Roger came from inside the house or outside. Roger came and put out the fires, and Howard knew then how much he needed Roger.

Howard needed Roger so much that he let Roger stay, even though Roger scared him nearly as much as the firebombs. If cocaine was making Howard fearful and timid, it was making Roger fearful and destructive, and Howard could never tell what would set him off. Sometimes they would be talking, laughing, and Roger's eyes would bulge, as though he had seen his own demons, and he would pound his fists and scream and fire his gun into the ceiling or the walls.

Once, Roger was talking to the girl who came to sleep with him and Howard saw the look in Roger's eyes, suddenly, too late. Roger hit the girl in the face with his fist. He kept hitting her, harder, until she collapsed, bloodier than Howard had ever seen a living person. Howard was so scared then that he didn't try to help her. Howard didn't say a word.

That frightened Howard more than Roger ever did. Howard always believed he put others first, that he would always help people who couldn't help themselves, but now that wasn't true. He could have helped Roger's girlfriend, but he would not take the risk. He would not risk being hurt, and he would not risk losing Roger's protection and he would not risk losing Roger's cocaine. The great strength of the ponytailed gladiator was gone for a lie. The cocaine that made him feel so much stronger was really making him weaker all the time, so weak he could not help himself, much less others.

Howard found out how helpless he was the night he and Roger brought two hookers home from a massage parlor. Howard paid for their services with a credit card. Howard and Roger promised them cocaine, but as soon as Roger walked through the door of Howard's house, he turned and screamed. He told the women to get out, and they ran. Roger slammed the door and then he slammed Howard against a wall.

Roger picked up one of his guns and pushed the barrel hard into Howard's mouth. Who did Howard think he was, bringing strangers into the house? Roger slid a trembling finger across the trigger, and Howard believed he was going to die.

Howard thought he had tasted death before, when he stuffed the bloody shirt in his mouth, but that was not this taste. This death tasted metallic, and burnt and dirty. Howard gagged, and Howard knew this was a gun that had been fired before.

Howard didn't know much about guns, but he knew about this gun. It was a Mac-10, a favorite of the Colombian drugsters. It was rapid-fire fast and deadly but not very accurate, except when the barrel was forced down the victim's throat. A light push on the trigger would touch off a dozen lethal explosions in less time than it took to sneeze, in less time than it would take for Howard's head to burst like a water balloon.

He thought about that as Roger screamed and sniffed and twitched, as he watched Roger's eyes try to push their way out of his head. He thought about running away. If he could get the gun out of his mouth, if he could somehow distract Roger for a moment, he could run. It was just a few yards to the window. He could take a chance on being cut by glass rather than blown apart by bullets, but he didn't.

Howard left it up to Roger to decide whether he would live or die.

Howard did not understand as much about Roger as he should have, as he would have without cocaine, but he decided this: Roger would rather scare him than kill him. If he ran, if Roger thought, even for moment, that he would never scare Howard again, Roger would pull the trigger for sure. So Howard stayed and tasted the dirty metal that cut his gums and waited for Roger to let him go, and Roger did. Howard did not run away, even then.

Even then, Howard waited for Roger to share more cocaine. Even then, Howard believed that Roger would protect him. He was too scared and too weak to believe anything else.

It did not occur to Howard that if Roger were really protecting him, the man with the shotgun could not have walked into his bedroom, or that the firebombs would never have reached his living room. It did not occur to Howard that a man with a shotgun standing over him while he slept could not have missed his head, unless he wanted to.

It did not occur to Howard that Roger was his ugliest demon.

Howard believed what he wanted to believe, as he always did, and Roger made sure that Howard stayed too scared to change his mind. Roger swore he would stop the man who was trying to kill Howard, and Howard went limp every time Roger said the name: Barry Hunwick.

The name was in the papers now, all the time. The papers said Barry Hunwick killed more people than anyone ever had for money, and that he worked for the biggest drug dealers in the country. The police never tried to prove it. It was hard to find witnesses, and harder still to find witnesses who would talk. The detective who said Hunwick killed 300 people was reprimanded and kicked off the case. The police finally charged Hunwick with just one murder, but that would be enough to send him to prison for many years if they could convict him. It was enough to worry Barry Hunwick, and the people he worked for, and his former lawyer, Andy Mavrides.

Before he disappeared, Andy startled his neighbors by running through his house, from window to window, shouting that someone was trying to kill him. He told his friends that he started getting threats soon after he started to represent Hunwick. Callers wanted to know what his client had told him, and what his client might be tempted to tell a judge to make a deal. Andy told his friends he was scared, and then, like so many witnesses, he was gone.

Hard as it was, the police did find a few people who would talk about Hunwick, people in enough trouble to want to save themselves from going to prison. One of them turned out to be a cocaine dealer named Linda, whose former boyfriend was a ponytailed drug lawyer named Howard Finkelstein.

Howard never loved Linda. When they dated, Howard

thought only about sex and cocaine, but both were available elsewhere in abundance and Howard didn't think it would matter so much when he broke off with her. It mattered to her. One day when Howard was at work, Linda broke into his house and emptied every drawer and every closet and tore up everything Howard owned. Then she wrote a note telling him how much she hated him, and how much she wanted him dead. She wrote it in lipstick, on the wall.

When Howard thought about Linda and about Barry Hunwick, he believed everything Roger said. It was easy to believe that Hunwick would kill him, or have him killed, thinking it would keep Linda quiet. It was easy to believe he would kill both of them on the chance that she had told Howard too much. It was easy to believe Linda was saying terrible things about Howard to anyone who would listen.

Howard needed Roger to protect him, and that is all Roger wanted. Roger always leaned close when he talked to Howard, as though he didn't want anyone else to hear, even though there was no one else in the room. Roger always leaned close and told Howard they needed each other because there was no one else to trust, and that Howard would never have to worry, but Howard wasn't sure.

"What if you're not here?" he asked. "What if they find me alone? How can I stop them?"

Roger didn't answer. Roger handed Howard a gun, and Howard took it.

If there is one moment that Howard can point to as the moment he went mad, it was the moment he took the gun. It was a handgun, a small one. Howard didn't know the make or the size, but it didn't matter and it didn't matter that Howard only carried it for a few days or that he never pulled the trigger. A hippie does not carry a gun. The moment he took the gun, Howard killed the hippie and the little fat boy and the idealistic young lawyer. Howard had become everything he hated, except rich.

He followed Roger everywhere, and Roger followed him. Howard was afraid to go to work in the morning, and stayed away for days. He made excuses to his clients and his partners and his friends. He lied to every one of them so he could sit for days in his chair smoking cocaine, but now, even freebase couldn't hide him for long.

At first, climbing so high and fast, Howard felt dizzy and tense, like a nervous flier on a great jet straining to take off and climb above the clouds. By the second day, he felt better, stronger, clearer. He let the chair carry him, and he did not worry about falling out. But by the third day, he was tense again, clutching the arms and breathing heavy. Cocaine is not like a jet plane that climbs above the clouds and levels off and settles into a soft, humming path. Cocaine is a rocket that goes up or down, as fast one way as the other. Howard was always afraid to fall, so he kept going up, kept smoking more and more, but he was afraid of that, too.

By the third day, Howard heard only the sounds of his mind. He could not hear Roger or anyone else. He could see lips move, and sometimes he could see the words tumble out and spill across the floor, but he could not hear them. He could hear nothing until the fourth day, when he would hear the little men running past in the dark, little men so fast they were invisible. Howard could never make out what they were saying, but Howard could hear them talking. Howard could hear them talking about him. He could not see them, but he could see electricity shooting out of the wall sockets. He could see it shoot across the room, in front of his eyes, and he kept ducking to avoid it, just fast enough each time.

All this time, Howard did not sleep and he did not eat and he did not wash himself. He left the chair to go to the bathroom, when he could find the bathroom, and came right back. All this time, Howard could not think of coming down, back through the noise of little men, back through the bolts of electricity from the walls. Coming down meant falling down, falling off a rocket. That is the only way Howard could describe it: falling, crashing, dying. It was that painful, that impossible to think about.

But by the fifth day, he did think about it. He thought about it because, by the fifth day, it was just as painful to go higher, just as impossible. By the fifth day, he did not care if he died.

The fall was always as awful as Howard imagined, except that he did not die, and that meant he would go up again. That meant he would go on lying and go on living in a house with bullet holes in the walls and television sets in the garage.

He rushed back to that house every day after work, when he went to work, and whenever Roger left, Howard left too. Roger never left the house without at least three guns, including an Uzi submachine gun.

One night Howard went with Roger to a motel where Roger had drug business. Howard waited in the car. Roger went into a room carrying the canvas bag he always carried, the bag filled with guns and drugs, and came out with nothing more that Howard could see. Roger drove away in a rush. Later, Roger took something from the bag that Howard had never seen before, something lumpy and gray: plastic explosives.

A few days later, Howard went to work and found a bundle of butcher paper on the doorstep. He opened it and saw a fish. Howard thought that was funny, until he thought about it more, and then he thought it was funnier. He had seen the movies, bad movies, where mob thugs sent dead fish to people they were going to kill. Even a paranoid cocaine addict could tell it was a joke. But what was the funny part? Howard thought about it all day, and then he wasn't sure it was funny at all.

The next day, two men Howard didn't know came to the office asking for him. They were big men, good-looking and clean and well-dressed. They said they were in the fish business. They told Howard they worked for the man Roger did business with in the motel that night, and Howard knew the man's last name immediately. It was the name of a Mafia family. The men told Howard that Roger cheated their boss. Roger had not paid for the plastic explosives and the machine gun and whatever else was in the bag. They wanted Howard to pay.

The men knew all about Roger's business and they knew he lived in Howard's house, and they knew all about Howard, the big-shot drug lawyer. They told Howard that as long as he was protecting Roger, he was responsible for his debts. They wanted $25,000.

Howard heard the words over and over: The men thought he was protecting Roger. That's what they thought, because that's what Roger told them. Finally Howard understood: Roger had been using him all along. Roger wasn't protecting him at all.

Now Howard had no one to protect him, and everyone to fear. He could not confront Roger, because he was afraid Roger would kill him. He could not call the police, because he was afraid the police would arrest him for his drug use. And he could not pay these men. Howard the big-time drug lawyer hadn't saved a dime. The men told him he could have a few days to get the money, no more. When they left, Howard left, too. He went straight to his father's house.

Howard was always welcome at his father's house. Maury Finkelstein was proud of his son and hardly blind to his problems. He had met Roger, and he saw the bullet holes in the walls. He had tried to talk to Howard, to help him understand that he had lost the path, but Howard did not want to hear him, and Maury did not want to lose Howard. No matter how sick or angry Howard was, he was always welcome at his father's house.

Marilyn welcomed him, too. She was not old enough to be his mother, but she loved him enough. Howard was a pot-smoking hippie of 19 when Maury moved back to Hollywood and married Marilyn. She treated him like one of her own. She was just as proud as Maury when Howard became a lawyer and won all those good fights. She read the stories and showed them off and showed him off, too. Marilyn could never be angry with Howard, but she was angry about what was happening to Howard. Maury and Marilyn would do anything to help, and Howard knew that.

Howard went to his father's house and told Maury about the men and the fish, and Maury knew Howard was scared because he would not stay in the house. Howard did not want his demons to find him there, because he did not want anything to happen to Maury. Howard asked his father to help, and then he went into the backyard to sleep in the bushes.

Maury promised to help his son, and he did. Maury had done well in real estate for the same reasons Howard had done well in law: He was smart, and he could get along with anyone. A lot of the people Maury got along with were the sort of people who needed lawyers, the sort of people who knew how to get money and how to get things done. Maury started calling them to ask if they knew the man who wanted Howard's money. One of them did. A few days later, the men from the fish business showed up at Maury's office.

Howard's father was not afraid of these men. He turned on a tape recorder under his desk before they began to talk. He told them that his son was not the one who cheated their boss, and he told them to leave Howard alone. He told them he would go to the police. They told him that if he did, they would ruin his son. They told him what they knew about Howard and cocaine, and they told him they would make sure the state attorney heard all about it, the state attorney and the Florida Bar. Maury told them he was done talking to them. He asked to see their boss. They promised to give him the message, and left.

Maury went home and told Howard he was taking care of everything and thought the trouble would be over soon. He told Howard not to worry, but Howard had already stopped worrying.

He had already called Roger to bring cocaine.

Settling accounts

The restaurant was small, a family place on Hallandale Beach Boulevard not far from Gulfstream race track, with clean, white tablecloths. The food, Italian, was very good.

The waiter led Maury and Howard to a room in the back, where an old man in a sport jacket and summer shirt, open at the collar, sat at the head of a long table. He gestured for them to sit, and waited for the others to join them, on the other side.

Joe Puma spoke softly, and he told everyone he expected them to do the same. He was the mob boss of South Broward, the man who ran the men who ran the gambling houses and whorehouses and all the rest. He did not have to raise his voice. He would listen to both sides and decide who was right, and there would be no appeal.

The man who demanded justice from Howard sat to Puma's left. He explained how Roger cheated him, and his voice rose as he blamed the punk lawyer. The old man told him to quiet down, but Howard jumped up. Maury reached up and pulled his son back into his chair. "Listen," he said, "and be quiet."

When it was Howard's turn, Maury spoke first. He explained that his son was a victim, and that he meant no harm to these men, and he thanked the old man for listening. Then Howard spoke, the way Howard spoke in court. He spoke about justice and fairness and he looked the old man in the eye.

"The fact that you are listening tells me you are a fair man," he said.

Puma smiled, and then he asked everyone to leave. He called Maury the next day with the verdict: Howard was not completely at fault, but he was not completely innocent. He was to pay $5,000. Maury thanked him, and sent the money right away. Howard paid his father back with the money from his next two cases.

Now Howard felt safe again, safe enough to forget everything. Now he knew it was never Barry Hunwick who was after him, and he had taken care of the men who were. He was certain they held no grudge when Maury got a call a few days after he sent the money. The old man was thinking of selling the restaurant, and he wanted Maury to be his agent.

Howard thought it was time to go back home, back to Roger, who brought him cocaine when he needed it. He wanted to go back, but this time, Maury and Marilyn stopped him. They kept him in their house, night and day, talking until he started to listen, and to sweat. He needed to see that Roger was not his friend, and that cocaine was killing him. He needed to tell Roger to get out of that house, but Howard said he could never do that. Marilyn said she could. Marilyn is a sweet, red-haired woman who can smile at anything except when her children are in danger. When Roger called for Howard, Marilyn answered and told the son of a bitch to clear out. She may not have scared Roger, but she scared Howard. He told her never to talk like that to a man who carries a gun.

Howard called Roger and apologized, but Roger told him it wasn't necessary. "Don't worry about your parents causing us trouble," Roger said. "I know where to find them."

Howard heard it echo: "I know where to find them." And Howard knew then that Maury and Marilyn were right. But now what could he do?

"Go away," Maury said. "Go away for a couple of months, long enough for Roger to think you're gone for good. He has nothing to gain by hurting us. When he thinks you're gone, and when he's gone, you can come back. And while you're gone, you can get better, and when you come back, there will be nothing to be afraid of."

This time, Howard could not argue. He was too scared, for his parents and for himself. Howard did not want to go to a treatment center for drug addicts because he did not believe he was a drug addict and he did not want to stop using cocaine, but he knew it was the one place Roger would not find him. Howard went away, and after a while, Roger stopped looking. When they turned the electricity off, Roger moved out. The house was ruined.

Maury and Marilyn stood by Howard while he tried to get well, and so did his partners. Howard lived for weeks in a place that was cool and quiet, except for the screams. The treatment was nothing remarkable, nothing he couldn't have received at any of the other private clinics that were opening across South Florida like fast-food restaurants along a new highway.

At least this was a comfortable place, like a summer camp for drug addicts, in white-wood cottages near the beach. Some of the others were more like hospitals, or hotels or insurance offices. Addicts with money, or insurance, could take their choice. They could have pastel walls or white, and carpet or tile, and tennis courts or sandy parks or nature trails. They could vomit wherever they wanted.

Howard did not vomit at all. Howard was an addict, but Howard was addicted only to cocaine, and cocaine does not kick its lovers in the stomach when they try to leave. Cocaine is meaner than that: It left Howard's body, but not his mind. In a few days, when his blood ran clear of drugs, the therapists began talking, but Howard did not hear them. He was too tired and too sad, and they would not let him have the only thing that would make him strong and happy.

"You are a drug addict," the therapists said, and Howard nodded, because he knew that is what they wanted.

"You are a drug addict and you will always be a drug addict and you will have to struggle every day to stay clean and straight."

Howard nodded, and he wondered what they were talking about. Why would he struggle at all? He had gone overboard with freebase, he thought, but who wouldn't with all his problems? Now that he was rid of those, cocaine would be no problem at all.

Howard nodded politely and thanked everyone for being concerned.

When Howard was released from the center after six weeks, he moved into a different house in a different neighborhood. It was a lot like the old house, but clean and strong, just like Howard. It was the perfect place for a new start and a new life. He even had a new phone number, so no one from his old life would find him.

It was weeks before Roger came knocking on Howard's new door.

Losing his balance

Soon after Judy Stern became Howard's secretary, soon after he came back from treatment, she learned to lock the door when she left the office. She learned to lock Howard in.

It didn't do much good, because he could always unlock the door from inside, or climb out the window, but she felt better knowing she tried. At the very least, she said to Howard: "Stay here."

If she fell for the earnest look in his little-boy eyes and told him it was all right to leave, Howard would disappear. Judy could never tell when he'd be back, or if he'd be back, but she could count on this: Howard would be high.

His time in treatment was not entirely wasted, because Howard stopped taking cocaine for a while, but not a long while. Howard didn't want to stop. Howard decided that he had a freebase problem, not a drug problem, and he looked to drugs for a solution.

Until he went to the clinic, Howard had not lived through a day without marijuana since he was 16, and he did not think his life improved in the weeks without it. Howard started to smoke marijuana again and he swallowed Percodan.

Howard did not see anything wrong with swallowing Percodan. Howard got his first prescription for Percodan in his freshman year in college, when he slid head-first into second base during a baseball game with friends. Howard grabbed his neck and screamed. An X-ray showed fused vertebrae, and the doctor said Howard was probably born that way.

"Don't slide head-first into second base," the doctor said, "and take these, whenever you need to."

Howard had never been a drinker, except when he went to the bars with his lawyer friends, but he started drinking martinis and beer at lunch, to carry him along until his afternoon pills and pot. The effect was soothing, warming, like an old blanket. On the days without cocaine, Howard wrapped himself in the old blanket and pulled it up over his head.

No longer electrified by the lightning that shot from his nose to his brain, or by the furious bolts from the wall sockets, Howard floated along, smiling and satisfied, convinced he was cured. His new secretary was not. Judy had known Howard for years, since they worked together in the public defender's office, and she admired him for his good work and his good heart, but he never fooled her.

She told Howard from the start that she would not waste her time working for a man who lacked the self-respect to put his job ahead of his selfish indulgences. Howard told Judy how much he needed to hear that, how much he needed someone like her to kick him in the ass and keep him pointed in the right direction. Howard meant every word he said, and he meant none of them. Even at his worst and weakest, Howard craved approval, and he craved Judy's, because he respected her. More than that, he craved her help, and he knew she was too good a person to turn him down.

Howard did not fool Judy, but Judy fooled herself. She gave Howard the help he wanted, but it was really no help at all, except to Howard the addict. Judy thought that Howard could stand up against his habits if she could keep the pressures of everyday life from knocking him down. She was wrong.

As long as Howard could stand, with the help of his parents and Judy and his partners and all the other people who cared about him, Howard could see nothing wrong. He could see nothing wrong with his habits, and he could see nothing wrong with taking advantage of good people.

Howard could have been Judy's brother. They were the

same height, the same weight, they had the same fair, straight hair, except that Judy's was cropped close around her tortoise-shell glasses. But Howard became more of an adopted son, although they were nearly the same age. Howard was like a scruffy little boy that Judy found on a street corner and brought home. In some ways, he was like a scruffy little boy from another planet. Judy was amazed at all the things Howard could not do.

The great lawyer could not balance a checkbook. He could not pay his bills, even if he had the money, and he had no idea if he had the money. Among his unpaid bills were traffic tickets, and his driving record was worse than some of his clients'. He would see his clients only when he remembered, but he rarely remembered. Unlike Channing and his new partner, Ron Dallas, Howard could not keep an appointment book, and he could not function without one. When he did show up, he stank.

Howard's body had become a chemical dump, and when it was full, the poison spilled out of his organs and leaked through his skin. It didn't matter that he bathed every day, except the days when he was lost to cocaine, or that he washed his long hair and combed it straight and free and cinched it with a rubber band, just as he did in high school. Howard smelled as though he still lived in his car, eating dog food.

Judy was amazed that for all this, people kept coming in and dumping money on Howard's desk.

Howard may not have been organized or studious or dependable, but his name still drew clients, big and small. The first change Judy made was to stop the money before it got to Howard. She counted it, wrote out receipts and took it to the bank. She kept two checkbooks in her desk: the office account, and Howard's personal account. His personal account carried Judy's name, too. She wrote out the checks for the business, and then she paid Howard's bills and his traffic tickets.

She did not give Howard a paycheck, because he did not know what to do with one. Once a week, she gave Howard an allowance, just enough to put gas in the car and buy lunch. If he wanted more, he had to have a reason. Howard was 30 years old and if he wanted to go out on a date, he had to ask Judy for an advance on his allowance. Judy made all of Howard's appointments, and she made sure he kept them. If he couldn't, or wouldn't, Judy made sure someone else did.

For a while, Judy believed it was working, for the while that Howard stayed away from the worst drugs. When Howard was sober, he did exactly what Judy told him to do, and he did a terrific job. Judy had worked with other lawyers who shared Howard's impatience with homework, but she had never worked with one who could do so little and still do so well. She would hand Howard the police report on a client and watch him read it until he smiled. Then Howard would look up and tell Judy his defense: the police search was illegal, the evidence was tainted, the client was an innocent bystander. For most cases, the drug cases, that's all it took. Howard knew how juries thought, he knew how the judges thought, and he knew the law.

Judy listened to Howard talk to his clients, and believed even more that she was right to help him. She heard them offer Howard drugs, and she heard him turn them down. She heard them tell him they were framed, she heard him say this: You can't fool me. I'm a drug addict, too.

Judy believed that if Howard could admit that, to himself and others, he was determined to quit. She knew he hadn't succeeded. When he started taking Percodan or other pills, she could tell, and she would tell him to cut it out. Howard would promise, again and again, and Judy believed he was trying. She was gentle with Howard, like a mother who did not want her troubled son to run away, until she caught him lying, again and again.

One afternoon, she walked into Howard's office and found him asleep on the couch, with his shoes off. One shoe caught her eye, the one with the bag of marijuana stuffed inside. Judy did not wake him right away. Judy had a starter's pistol, and she put it on Howard's desk. She put the bag of marijuana next to it, and she laid out paper and pen. Then she woke Howard.

"Write out your will," she ordered, "and then finish yourself off with the gun. You are making everyone else miserable watching this slow death of yours. Go ahead and shoot yourself."

Howard didn't shoot himself. Howard promised to be good.

Mothering Howard wasn't so hard at first, writing out a few checks and keeping his tie straight and fishing the rotted sandwiches and dirty laundry from his car. It got harder when Howard went back to cocaine. Then, there was nothing anyone could say to Howard or do for Howard or do to Howard that could keep him on his feet for long.

When Howard went to look for cocaine, Judy went looking for Howard. She got to know his old friends, his cocaine friends, and their haunts. Whenever Judy lost Howard, she spent her day, or night, looking through bars and boatyards. Sometimes she needed help to find him or to bring him back. Judy joined with Howard's family to watch him or search for him around the clock. Between Judy and Maury and Howard's brother Ricky, someone always found him, eventually.

Judy and Maury and Ricky and Howard's partners all agreed on this: Howard's old friends were his biggest problem. If he could stay away from them, he could stay away from drugs. They did not want to consider the other possibility: that if he could stay away from drugs, he would stay away from his old friends.

One day, when they found Howard stoned, his partners threw him in a car and drove him to a ranch in far-west Davie, a cow town on the edge of the Everglades. The woman who owned the ranch was a warm and wise friend who agreed to keep Howard where he could inhale nothing more exhilarating than fresh air and cow manure. She knew a lot about drugs and danger. She was Barry Hunwick's mother-in-law. When Howard was sober enough to listen, she gave him a long lecture about his folly and told him he was welcome to stay and get well. Howard liked her. Howard liked her so much he went back to visit many times, but he did not like her enough to stay.

He did not like anyone enough to stay away from cocaine for long.

Howard did not even stay away from freebase for long, but he does not know how long and it doesn't matter. Whether it was days or weeks or months after he got out of treatment, it happened, and he could not help himself. Once he opened the door to cocaine, he did not want to close it. When Howard saw the lightning, he wanted to feel the thunder, and he rushed out into the storm. He rushed to Jeff's house.

Howard rushed to Jeff's house and smoked cocaine and lost himself, for days, but it was different this time. This time, it was harder to fly above the anxiety, the tension, the fear, because this time, Howard knew that he was getting lost and he knew what happened the last time he was lost, and it scared him. Howard did not want to be lost where Roger could find him. He did not know that Roger was already looking.

When Howard moved into his new house, Judy had his phone number listed under a different name, a name that showed she believed in him and that Howard could still believe in himself. She had his new phone listed under the name Peter Pan. Roger didn't bother looking it up.

Roger had a lot of customers in a lot of places, and Roger's customers did whatever Roger wanted. One of them worked for the telephone company. She helped Roger do favors for other people who paid him money. Through her, Roger could find out if someone's phone was being tapped and he could trace calls and he could get unlisted phone numbers. He could also find out where the bills were being mailed for a man named Howard Finkelstein, no matter how he was listed.

Howard did not open the door when he saw Roger. Howard told him to go away, but Roger did not go anywhere. "I don't want to come in," he said. "I just want to tell you something important. Someone is trying to kill you."

How could he do this again? How could he think that Howard the lawyer, Howard the gladiator, would listen to this and believe? Roger was not speaking to Howard the lawyer or Howard the gladiator. Roger was speaking to Howard the drug addict, and Howard the drug addict did not turn away, even as his palms began to sweat, even as his heart began to pound.

Howard the drug addict needed to hear more: "Who is trying to kill me?"

That was all Roger needed to hear. He mentioned a name, and then other names. He talked about the case Howard was working on, and told him things anyone could know from looking up the records, but he also told him things that weren't in any record. He told Howard just enough to make him open the door, and that was all Roger wanted.

Roger always knew just enough. Roger always knew just enough to make Howard believe or make Howard scared or make Howard forget the awful things that always happened when he listened to Roger. Roger knew just enough to make Howard open the door, and when he did, Roger walked in carrying his canvas gym bag.

Roger walked into Howard's new house talking about Howard's new case, and while he talked he took a tall, glass pipe out of his bag. Roger's crack pipe looked like a Sultan's pipe, like the fat-bottom hashish pipes of the Arabian nights, but it was all clear glass, even the mouthpiece, with no braided hose or brass fittings or gold-leaf filigree, with nothing to obscure the pure and white and hypnotic smoke of cocaine.

Roger had already cooked his cocaine into rocks and he laid them on the mesh screen and set them on fire. Howard listened, and Howard watched. Howard listened to the sound of cocaine frying, and he heard nothing else. He watched the cloud swell and fill the glass and rub itself against the glass walls, and he wanted nothing except to breathe it in, and he did, and it was gone.

Roger's pipe was not like a hashish pipe because crack cocaine is not like hashish. Crack cocaine is not sweet and thick and it does not linger in the mouth and rise slowly through the lungs. Crack cocaine is sharp and quick, like a bullet. Howard breathed in Roger's cocaine and his mind exploded.

Howard could feel the explosion even before it happened, even as he watched the cocaine smoke fill the glass pipe, even as he watched Roger place the rocks on the screen. It was an explosion powerful enough to make him forget that this man hurt him and that this man threatened to hurt his parents and that this man took over his house and his life. Howard did not remember any of it until Roger was gone.

When Roger was gone and Howard finally crashed, Howard remembered it all and he swore it would not happen again, and it didn't, for a while. The next time Roger came back, Howard did not open the door, until Roger said they needed to talk, until he saw that Roger was carrying the canvas bag, and then it happened the same way, again. There were times, after that, when Howard called Roger, even though he hated him, even though he began to sweat as soon as he reached for the phone, even though he felt his heart kicking the walls of his chest as he stood by the window, waiting.

The people who cared about Howard, and people who didn't really care at all, told him the same thing: "Get away from Roger." Sometimes, Howard listened. Twice, he listened to other cocaine friends who said they could force Roger to leave. We are your real friends, and we will protect you, they said. It did not occur to Howard that this is exactly what Roger said, and that they were no different. Howard told them to send Roger away, but Roger sent them away instead. Roger was meaner and Roger was smarter and Roger knew Howard better than all of them. Roger always knew just enough to make Howard scared.

If Roger wouldn't leave, Howard could, and Judy and his partners tried to make him. They sent him away on vacations, to stay with friends, while they tried to think of ways to sober him up when he returned. Howard was away when Roger got arrested.

A policeman spotted the expired license plate and signaled Roger to pull his green-and-white Buick to the side of State Road 7 in Hacienda Village, a tiny, trailer-park speed trap without so much as a roadside diner. When Roger opened the glove box to get the registration, the policeman saw the gun: a blue-steel, .22-caliber North American Arms five-shot handgun, loaded and cocked. The officer drew his own gun and pulled Roger out of the car.

A search of Roger's car and travel bag turned up two more guns, a Beretta .380 and a Walther PP. They also found $2,355.60 in cash and an assortment of pills, and cocaine. Roger was arrested and taken to the county jail, where he gave Howard's address as his own and listed his occupation as self-employed investigator. He had enough money to post bond, even though his damned attorney was nowhere to be found. Roger was out of jail just long enough to rearm himself and replenish his traveling drug supply before being arrested again the next day a few miles away. This time, it took longer to bail out, long enough to let Judy try to keep him out of Howard's house for good.

Ricky went through the place, to be sure Roger wasn't around, and Judy called a locksmith. The next day, with Ricky inside to guard the house, Roger came pounding on the door. He wanted his guns. Ricky refused to open the door, and Roger went away. Late that night, Judy's unlisted phone rang, and she thought it might be Howard. It was Roger, with a short message: "Don't get in my way, or else". A few days later, on her way to work, a car suddenly pulled in front of Judy's and forced her off the road. When Howard returned from vacation, Judy rushed to tell him everything, and Howard was not surprised.

Howard knew too much to ever be surprised by Roger again. Howard knew that Roger was not his friend, but Howard still wanted Roger's cocaine too much to believe that Roger was his enemy.

"I'll deal with Roger," he told Judy, but he was not ready for that, and Judy knew it.

The next time Howard was missing, Judy went to his house, but she did not find Howard or Roger. She found a strange man asleep on Howard's bed, holding a shotgun in his arms. Roger sent this man to stay in Howard's house to guard his guns and his drugs, and to keep people like Judy from causing trouble. Before she left, Judy scooped up the drugs lying out on the tables and threw them in the garbage.

The only thing Judy could think to do was keep sending Howard out of town, hoping each time that he would come back sober and realize what an awful mess he had made. She did not know how awful it had become.

Now that Howard took him back, Roger wanted more than legal advice and a spare garage. One night, as they snorted cocaine, Roger asked Howard to help him kill a man.

Roger wanted to kill Howard's friend Jeff, the one who taught him how to freebase.

Jeff and Roger had become partners, but hardly equals. Howard was kept out of their drug deals, because they needed him to be their lawyer, but he knew Roger wasn't satisfied. Roger resented Jeff's million-dollar home, and his chalet at Lake Tahoe. He told Howard he wanted to make one last deal, and he wanted Howard to set it up. He wanted Howard to meet Jeff at Lake Tahoe and take him to a place where Roger could shoot him in the back.

This was the lowest moment of Howard's life, worse than the moment he took Roger's gun. He listened to Roger talk about murder and did not curse him or throw him out or call the police. That is the moment that makes Howard certain he lost his soul.

He listened to Roger talk about murder, and all he could think about was cocaine.

Sharing the blame

Donna thought it was her fault.

Howard called when he got home from Las Vegas, where she took his picture at the lawyers' seminar, and he called again, often. She was perfectly happy with the man who lived with her, but she could not resist the charm of her old class rival. There was no telling when he would call, but whenever he did, Howard was exciting to hear. Even over the phone, there was power in his voice and passion in his words. Donna admired Howard's success as a lawyer, fighting for the poor, just as she had admired him in political science class.

Then why did he stop calling?

"It is my fault," Donna thought. "It is my fault because I could not make up my mind about him, and now he is gone."

It made Donna angry, as much as it made her sad. Donna did not like to think of herself as weak and indecisive. Donna was bold and sure and adventurous, and she proved it, over and over. She proved it to Howard when he came to visit.

When Howard flew to Las Vegas to see Donna, she took him hiking in the mountains. Howard wanted to stop long before she did. When they sat to rest and Howard lit a cigarette, Donna took an ashtray out of her sack. "And be careful where you sit," she said, "so you don't hurt the plants."

"What an amazing woman," Howard thought. All the time he spent in the courtroom Donna had spent exploring the woods and the roads and the country. She loved white-water rafting and water skiing. She had even jumped out of an airplane. Donna was as determined to cut her own path as Howard was to follow his. Donna had a spirit of adventure, and a confidence to follow it that excited Howard as much as he excited her.

After college, Donna had explored the business world just as she explored the woods, but it wasn't nearly as much fun. She went to work in the office of a large supermarket chain. Then she decided to study to become a stockbroker, and took a job as administrator of a finance company. No matter what she tried, Donna hated working in offices, for corporations.

She hated the politics. She hated supervising people who couldn't do their jobs, almost as much as she hated working for people who couldn't do their jobs. She hated working for men who thought so little of women. Most of all, she hated doing work that didn't seem to help anyone accomplish anything. Donna took as job as a waitress and moved to a mountaintop near Tucson, Arizona.

Donna liked being on a mountaintop. She felt closer to the earth, and closer to the sky, and she took neither for granted. Donna set aside whole days to watch the earth and sky, sitting under a waterfall.

Like Howard, Donna smoked pot, but never while she was doing a dozen other things, never when she was driving or working. Donna smoked pot when it was time to smoke pot, when everything else was done. Like Howard, Donna snorted cocaine, but not nearly as often. Once a month, perhaps. Like Howard, Donna was sure cocaine could not make her an addict.

By the time Howard came to hike with her, Donna felt her life was nearly perfect, and then he stopped calling, and she wondered.

Howard's last few calls were more exciting then ever, and more confusing. Howard wanted to see her. He wanted her to come back to Florida, to stay with him, but Donna wouldn't say yes. "Listen," Howard said, "I have to run, but think about it and I'll call you back." Donna thought, and waited, for a year and a half.

"It is all my fault," Donna told herself, but she could not know the real reason Howard never called back: Howard forgot. The only reason he hung up was that Roger was passing him the cocaine, and when it was finished, days later, Howard did not remember that he had called Donna at all. For a long time after, Howard did not remember very much of anything, except that men were trying to kill him.

Donna moved again after that, and she did not tell Howard where to find her. She wrote him a letter, with no return address, to wish him well, and left for San Francisco. It wasn't until Howard came back from treatment, until his mind was clear, for a little while, that he decided to find her. He called Donna's old boyfriend and found out where she was.

The next time Judy sent him out of town to dry out, Howard flew to San Francisco.

Donna did not know why he came, but she was thrilled. Howard was as exciting as ever, and he was generous and sweet and attentive. Wherever they went, Howard made a striking presence with his ponytail and lizard-skin boots and his stories about war and justice in South Florida. Wherever the party, Howard wanted to be there and be seen and be heard and be liked. He wanted Donna to share his cocaine. He wanted Donna to come back to Florida with him, and this time he didn't quit. He kept coming back until she said she would.

It wasn't until then, when Donna came to visit Howard in Florida in February, 1984, that she had any idea he had a problem. She did not like the strange men in his house, or anything about his house or the way he lived. She wondered what made him so different at home, and Howard tried to explain.

He told Donna about Roger and about his time in the treatment center. He told her he had a freebase problem, not a cocaine problem, but it was over. He told Donna a lot, but he did not tell her everything, not the worst of it.

Howard did not tell her Roger stole his soul. He did not tell her another man nearly died because of it. The day Roger asked Howard to help him kill Jeff was the day Howard should have stood up to Roger and thrown him out for good, but he didn't. Now Howard was too ashamed.

When Roger asked him to help kill Jeff, Howard took the coward's way out, the lawyer's way out. He waited all day, until the drug haze lifted just enough to let him think but before it went away completely and took his little courage. Then he argued just hard enough to make Roger doubt himself. Howard told Roger that murder was too dangerous, because even a dumb cop could figure out the connections. Everyone, including cops, knew Roger was living in Howard's house, and if Howard was seen with Jeff before he died, Roger would become the prime suspect. Howard asked Roger: "Why risk going to jail for the rest of your life? You are already making money with him. Don't be greedy."

Howard won the argument. It was the only time he argued for the life of a man who didn't know he was on trial. Howard won his friend's life, but he lost his soul. He could not tell Donna how low he had fallen, but he told her enough to send her away.

Donna told Howard that she would not move in until Roger was gone, but he told her he didn't have the heart to disappoint an old friend. Donna went back to California and Howard did not know what to do. Until Roger exploded again.

Ever since Howard let Roger into the new house, he told himself over and over: "This time, it is different." This time, Roger did not stay more than a few days at a time and he did not shove guns into Howard's mouth. This time, Roger did not fill Howard's garage with television sets or beat women bloody in Howard's living room. "This time," Howard thought, "I have him under control." All Roger did was light the pipe and pass it to Howard as they sat in their chairs, for days on end. They were sitting and smoking and watching a tape of The Who in concert when it happened. Howard loved that tape, and he did not understand why the screen suddenly went blank and collapsed, as though someone shot the television set. He turned to Roger, and he saw the gun, and he knew it was all happening again.

Howard flew to California the next day and told Donna he was ready to make the choice, if she would help. For the first time, Donna saw weakness in her gladiator, and it made her stronger.

All those years, she thought of Howard as surer and

stronger, but now it was different. Now Donna knew what she wanted, and how she wanted it all done, and Howard could either go along or go away. Donna wrote her conditions on paper, like a contract, and Howard accepted: no strangers in the house, no freebasing, no fooling around. For years, Howard was more afraid of Roger than anyone or anything in the world. Now, he was more afraid of losing Donna.

For all the women who had come and gone, all the singers and models and coke dealers and coke whores, for all the women in black-slit dresses, Donna was the first woman in years who reminded Howard of what he wanted to be. Sick as he was, sad as he was, weak as he was, there was still a spark deep inside Howard. Donna found it, and Howard was thankful. When he talked to Donna, Howard felt excited again about helping the poor and changing the world, even though he doubted now that he ever could. But Donna believed, because she did not know how sick he was, and the more she believed the more Howard started to believe again.

When Howard fell in love with Donna, he fell in love with the idea of being the ponytailed gladiator again. For a little while, he seemed to be.

The promise of Donna coming to live with him, the promise of doing good work, lifted Howard. He worked harder, he stayed straighter and he felt stronger. This time, it wasn't a lie. Donna made Howard strong enough to tell Roger to leave.

Howard did not really stand up to Roger, because he blamed Donna, but it still took more courage than Howard showed in years. He told Roger that he and Donna were moving into a new house and Donna insisted on being there alone. Howard would not have been surprised if Roger shot him, but Roger didn't shoot him and he didn't argue. Roger didn't say a word as he packed his pipe in the canvas bag and walked out.

Roger left, and Howard wondered. Roger had left before, and he always came back, and Howard always let him in. Every day, for a long time, Howard expected Roger to knock at his door, but Roger never did, and little by little, Howard started to believe he was free of his last demon.

With Roger gone and Howard working hard, Donna felt better than ever. She stayed for months, and all her doubts vanished. The longer she stayed, the more she loved Howard, and the more certain she was about staying. She had to be certain, not just because she was leaving a man she lived with for seven years. She had to be certain for her parents' sake.

Donna's parents had been living in Tucson, but if she were moving to Florida, she wanted them near by. She had already torn them from home once, and she would not do it again unless it was for good. After six months with Howard, she was certain enough to buy a house with him: three bedrooms, two baths, 1,546 square feet in a quiet suburb, for $92,000. When they were all settled, Donna went back out west for a week to gather her life and family.

Donna was never more certain, until she called Howard from the road to say she'd be home in a few hours. Howard did not sound excited. Howard sounded cold and distant, like a stranger.

When she arrived with her parents, Howard was colder still. Donna could not imagine what the problem was, and Howard would not tell her. Howard said there was no problem, and asked her to leave him alone. Donna settled her parents into a motel, then came back and tried again to talk to Howard, but he was stranger than ever. She left him in the living room and went to the kitchen to think. She took a package of vanilla ice cream out of the freezer and took a spoon from the drawer and started to fill a bowl. When she looked down, she stopped and bent close to the counter. She did not understand why there were black streaks in the ice cream.

It looked like fudge, but this was not fudge ice cream. She looked at the spoon and turned it over, and she suddenly threw it down in the sink.

The back of the spoon was caked in black, as though someone had been holding it over a flame—as though someone had been using it to cook his cocaine.

First poison, then suicide

Donna ran into the living room and shoved Howard out of his chair. When he got up, slowly, startled, Donna ran straight at him and knocked him over again onto the couch. Donna wanted to keep knocking him down, the way he knocked her down.

She cursed him, and she cried. The anger Donna felt toward Howard could not match the anger she felt toward herself. How could she have been so stupid? How could she have believed him? How could she have done this to herself, and to her parents?

The answer was in the little-boy eyes, the ones Howard practiced on Judy, the ones that never failed. Howard looked up at Donna and pleaded for another chance.

"I'm weak," Howard said. "I never meant to hurt you, but I can't help myself. I can't stand up to Roger and the others without you. You're the only one who can help me. You shouldn't have left me alone all that time."

Donna listened, and she couldn't believe it. Howard thought it was her fault? Howard had the nerve to blame Donna? "What an asshole," she thought. Donna wanted to leave him there, on his back, whining, but she didn't. She had moved her parents across the country and she had spent all her money and their money and she had already given up too much, too many times. She looked back into Howard's little boy eyes and let him know that life was going to be very different.

"Don't tell me to be your baby-sitter," she said. "And don't expect me to put up with your crap. I am not married to you, and I won't stay unless you prove you can be honest with me. Do you understand?"

Howard understood, and he surrendered. Howard really believed that he wanted Donna more than he had ever wanted Roger's cocaine, but he did not have to choose. All she wanted was for Howard to stop freebasing. Howard had already stopped once, and he was sure he could stop again, especially if it was the only way to keep Donna. Howard surrendered, and he believed.

Donna believed, too, for a long time to come. With Donna watching, Howard went to work regularly and looked very much the successful lawyer. With Donna watching Howard, Judy relaxed, and they all agreed to treat Howard like an adult as long as he acted like one. Judy stopped locking him in the office.

Donna watched, and Donna believed what she saw. Donna could see, first-hand, that Howard was doing the work he always talked about, still helping poor people, and she was sure he was on the right track.

But Donna did not hear the way Howard talked to poor people, and she did not know what he really thought about them. Howard thought they were guilty. He forced himself to take them on and go through the motions of defending them, but he did not believe in them any more. Howard once treated them like family, but now he treated them like a family obligation, like old relatives who had to be clothed and fed and kept alive out of obligation rather than love. Howard cut them off when they tried to tell him their problems, and he scolded them, like children, for knowing less than a lawyer knows about the courts. He went through the motions, but that wasn't enough. It is emotion, not motion, that made Howard a lawyer, and he had no emotion left.

Howard wanted the poor people out of the way to give him time for the rich people, the ones with cash to pay for Howard's new home and his snakeskin boots. Howard wanted the poor people out of the way, except when they could put him in the headlines again.

Former public defender hasn't shed longhair view

That was the headline on Howard's first newspaper profile after his treatment, after Donna moved in, but it never mentioned his addiction. The story recounted his deep commitment to the underclass. It did not mention drugs at all, except to repeat Howard's plea to legalize everything. There was no reason for the story, no fresh triumph or scandal, except that Howard charmed a new courthouse reporter with his old hippie-lawyer stories. Howard did not tell the new stories, the ones about men with guns or about crack cocaine. Howard decided to pretend none of that ever happened.

After that story, there were more. The papers started calling Howard for quotes again, about social services and the homeless. He was cheered, again, for taking on such unpopular cases as the teenage mother who killed her baby, and he found new demand for his expertise in pornography when a new sheriff started arresting video store owners.

Everyone who knew Howard told Donna how wonderful she was for him, and how wonderful he was for her. Howard had proved he could live without lying, and Donna married him on March 30, 1985, almost a year after his coke spoon soiled her ice cream.

The marriage was the sign that all of Howard's friends had been waiting for. It was the sign that Howard had finally grown up, and the sign that he was well, except for that damned neck problem, but thank God the pills eased his pain. The good feelings ran wide and deep. After the wedding, Howard even began talking to his mother again. After the wedding, Howard could get away with anything.

Howard burrowed into his old, warm blanket of pills and martinis every day, and it didn't kill him, no matter what the medical books say. Percodan is a painkiller full of oxycodone, a narcotic. It depresses the nervous system. It is dangerous to take too much, and even more dangerous to take any amount with alcohol. Too much can slow the heart, or speed the heart, or clamp down the chest muscles until it is almost impossible to breathe. Howard swallowed Percodan by the handful, and washed it down with martinis, but that was never enough. He still smoked a joint, or two, every afternoon, and again when he got home. Being married did not make Howard any more circumspect than when he was single, back when Judy chased him around the office Christmas party, in a room filled with police and prosecutors, trying to pull the joint out of his mouth. Howard lit up every afternoon, no matter who was in the office.

Still, he followed the rule he learned early: no cocaine before court. Percodan was all right when he needed it, because he had built up such tolerance, but he kept away from cocaine until nighttime, and that was fine with Donna. She was happy to join Howard, not every time, but often. Howard took her to parties with lawyers and drug dealers, and sometimes they had parties of their own, just the two of them. Howard and Donna snorted cocaine together, just like all the other young couples who had graduated from college dorms to the suburbs.

Then Donna stopped. One warm night in the first summer of their marriage, Donna's cocaine turned to poison in her lungs. Something enormous squeezed her head and pushed her down, while her heart tried to kick through her chest. Donna believed she was having a heart attack, and the panic made it all worse. Her mouth dried up and she panted and she fell to the floor, and still she wanted more cocaine. Something inside said: "Take more cocaine, and this will go away. Take more cocaine and get higher, or you will fall and die." Donna didn't listen. Donna closed her eyes and let herself fall and she lived.

Donna never took cocaine again.

For Donna, it was that simple. She didn't need counseling or treatment, and she didn't need to be locked in a room. Donna wasn't a drug addict, but Howard was. When Donna stopped cocaine, she started to understand that. She tried to tell Howard, but he wouldn't listen.

"You had one bad trip," he said. "That happens. Why are you overreacting? You just need to do it again."

Donna listened, and she realized: This is not Howard talking. Howard was too smart, too kind, too decent to want his wife to risk dying, or to take the risk himself. This is not Howard, this is a drug addict. Donna tried to make Howard listen, and she tried to get him to tell the truth. "If you can stop," she said, "do it. If you can't, admit it and get help."

But Howard lied, to himself and to his wife. Howard said he could stop, any time, but he wouldn't, no matter how much she wanted him to. Donna thought about leaving, and she thought about it more and more in the months ahead.

Maybe Howard really was getting worse, or maybe Donna was seeing more than she had ever seen, but Donna and Howard were not happy as their first anniversary approached. They argued, every day, about Howard's drugs, and Howard turned nasty. Howard started to believe that if Donna wouldn't join him, she was against him, even though he knew she loved him.

He had to know, because she stayed, despite the cost. Now when Howard disappeared, it was Donna who went to the bars and boatyards to look for him, and she lost her job because of it. When Donna married Howard, she went to work for a company that provided temporary office help, and she was supposed to spend her days selling the service to executives. Instead, she spent many days looking for her husband, and trying to get him sober, and she could not keep it up.

Donna wanted to leave, but she believed too much in herself. She believed she could not have been so wrong. She must have a purpose with this man, and it must be to help him. What else could she think? All her life, Donna had been needed, and she thought it was normal. Her parents needed her now because they were old, but they needed her just as much when they were young. Her father was a smart and wonderful man, but he lost his business because so much of the world puzzled him. Donna was always the one who understood whatever was wrong and fixed it. When she was a little girl and the television picture went fuzzy, her parents called Donna to fix it. When she was a little girl and her family was going away on vacation, Donna made the plane reservations.

Now Donna was grown up and she was married to a little boy and it was only natural for her to do everything for him, even if he was a drug addict. Donna thought Howard was like a little boy with a punctured inner tube who ran from grown up to grown up crying: "Blow it up! Blow it up!" Someone always did, and now it was Donna's turn.

So Donna stayed and she argued, but she couldn't win. No one could argue with Howard and win. She knew that, just as she knew it in college, when he won every debate. She knew it because she saw him in court, winning cases he should have lost. She knew it because every time she tried, Howard turned her arguments around and slapped her with them. He might as well have used the back of his hands, or his fists.

"Who are you to lecture me," he asked. "Who are you to tell me anything? You can't even hold a job."

Howard hurt Donna with words until she left him alone, and then he did what he wanted. Howard had nothing to fear now. Donna could have left, but she didn't, so Howard had no reason to hide his drugs or his anger. He used Donna's oven to cook his cocaine and harden it with baking soda into pebbles. Howard did not need go back to freebase because he had discovered crack.

Crack was just like freebase, but more convenient, easier to carry, sort of a traveling version, perfect for pocket or purse. It was also available at popular prices, in alleyways and burned-out buildings, but Howard did not need to go to those places because he did not have to worry about the money. Howard made his own crack from his own cocaine, and he smoked it in his own home. Crack or freebase, the effect was the same: madness. Howard put the pebbles in his pipe and demons leaped from the fire. Howard leaped, too, as electricity shot from the walls again, and Donna cried.

Donna cried for Howard and she cried for herself and she cried because she could not understand why no one else saw what was happening. When Howard came home with the Cadillac, Donna thought that was enough, that it was the great billboard of Howard's insanity and no one could miss it.

Howard spent all their money on cocaine and then he came home one night with a year-old Cadillac Eldorado Biarritz. It had a big chrome band across the roof and a grill the size of their couch. Howard got a deal from a client and he borrowed the money from his friends. Donna knew he was mad.

Howard in a Cadillac? Howard the hippie, the socialist, the ponytailed gladiator, driving a car built for robber barons? Donna wanted everyone to know and everyone to see, so they would understand, but they didn't. "What a wonderful car," they said. "It's about time Howard grew up."

Donna knew she wasn't the only one fed up with Howard's behavior, and she saw others backing away. Judy quit to work for another lawyer, because she could not keep Howard locked up any more and she could not keep running after him. Channing Brackey quit to work for the IRS. But when Donna went to other friends and to Howard's parents and to her own parents and told them her husband was a drug addict, she did not get the sympathy she expected. They all told her the same thing: Howard is different.

"Be patient," they said. "Try to show him some support. Besides, people said, he keeps winning in court, doesn't he? Who are you to say such things about the great lawyer?"

Donna heard it so often, she began to ask herself: "Who am I? Could I really be so wrong?" The newspapers that adored Howard Finkelstein were not yet filled with stories about crack addicts and crack houses and crack babies—or about crack lawyers. The parents and friends who loved Howard and Donna did not know about any of these things, and they did not see all that she saw, and they did not want to believe. Donna never felt so alone.

Even her father, the smartest man she had ever known, a pharmacist who knew about drugs, told her to be thankful for all the good in Howard and to try to ignore the bad. Even her mother told her to stand by, no matter what, and try to help as best she could.

"But mom," Donna said, "he lies to me!"

"Of course he lies," her mother said. "He's a lawyer."

When Donna had no one else to turn to, she left, for a while. She went back to Las Vegas, to the man she lived with before Howard, and told him everything. Did he think she was crazy? "No. Your husband is an addict. You can either live with that or leave him, but you can't change him." That was all Donna needed to hear. She flew back to Florida and told Howard she wanted a divorce.

A divorce? Even through the crack and Percodan and marijuana and whatever else Howard put in his mouth or nose that day, he heard the awful words. Howard had not been afraid because he did not believe she would really go, but he was wrong. He would rather face Roger's gun barrel. He begged Donna, and he promised he would do whatever she wanted. He would give up crack and cocaine and anything she asked. He would never be mean again, and he would never say mean things.

Donna is not stupid, and she never was. Donna knew that Howard lied, to himself and everyone else, and she knew he was a manipulative son of a bitch, but she loved him, and she couldn't pretend she didn't. She agreed to stay, but only as long as he stayed honest and sober. Howard promised, as he promised so many times before, and Donna believed him, because she wanted to. Donna believed him for weeks, until Jan. 28, 1986. The morning the space shuttle Challenger exploded, so did Donna.

Donna was in Howard's office, helping, as she did, with paperwork and files and phone calls. He was supposed to be in court. Donna went to Howard's desk and saw a piece of paper with the address of a motel, in his handwriting. Donna believed in Howard, but she did not trust him. She drove to the motel and found him with a woman, in the bar, high as ever. Howard started to explain, but Donna didn't bother with an argument she couldn't win. "You are out of my life," she said, and for the second time since high school, Howard was thrown out of his house.

This time, Howard did not go off to live with hippies. This time, Howard moved into a penthouse on the Intracoastal

Waterway, and he learned the wrong lesson, again. He learned that what he feared most could happen, and he would survive. He loved Donna, but if she didn't want him, others did. Howard moved in with a client's sister, and he let everyone know. He wanted Donna to be hurt, as if he hadn't hurt her enough.

Howard did hurt Donna, and so did their friends. The way Howard jumped into the high life of crack cocaine and all-night parties, the way he vanished for days, again, from his office and clients, Howard might as well have jumped off the penthouse balcony and taken his chances with the current below. Everyone blamed Donna.

"Didn't we tell you to be patient and try to help and try to understand that Howard is different?" they all said. "Didn't you know he had a problem?"

Donna knew only this: Howard lied and Howard hurt her and she could not make him stop. She had never been so depressed, or so confused. She was confused when the hospital called to say that Howard was there, with pneumonia. Donna took him back to her house and took care of him until he was rid of the pneumonia, but Howard still wasn't well, and he was meaner than ever. "This is all your fault," he said.

Donna had suffered enough, but she could not leave.

If she left him now, he would never see that he was wrong. If she left him now, everyone would blame her when he finally hit bottom. If she left him now, the pain would be all hers.

Donna could not leave, but she could not stay, so she decided to die. She could not think of anything that would hurt Howard more.

One day, when Howard went to work, or wherever Howard went when he said he was going to work, Donna took off all her clothes and hung them neatly and sat in the bathtub to kill herself. Donna had it all planned, so that she would leave no mess. She ran the water and slid down low and reached for the razor she always kept at the edge of the tub, but it wasn't there. Donna jumped up and pulled open the medicine chest. It wasn't there either. Donna could not think of anything else, and she started crying. She could not think of knives or poison or pills. She cried as she ran through the house, naked and dripping, pulling at drawers and cabinets and handbags and suitcases, but there wasn't a razor blade anywhere.

And then she remembered.

Donna had thrown out all the razor blades so that Howard could not cut his cocaine. Howard ruined her life, and now he was ruining her death. Donna stood there, and cried for a long time.

She was still crying when she went to the phone to call for help. She called Howard's partner, Ron Dallas, who did not blame her for hurting Howard. He dropped everything to help Donna, just as he had dropped everything to help Howard so many times, and took her to a hospital. She was still sobbing as she told the psychiatrist about Howard and his drugs and his criminal friends and his lies. The psychiatrist told her he understood, but he didn't.

The doctor was more impressed with her husband, the brilliant young attorney who was always in the newspapers. He was obviously no drug addict. Howard explained that Donna was a wonderful woman who suffered from delusions. He hoped and prayed that the doctor could help. The doctor assured Howard that women sometimes react hysterically to stress, and told him to be patient with her.

He prescribed Valium, and released Donna on one condition: She had to remain in Howard's care.

Killing Howard

Donna wanted Howard to die.

Each night, when the drugs finally dragged him down, when all the laughs and lies and meanness finally eddied and drained from his dry, useless body, when Donna finally felt free, for a little while, she stood over Howard and prayed that he would never get up again

Sometimes, when she wanted to believe her prayers were answered, she held a mirror under his nose to see if he was still breathing. She could not tell by watching his chest. Howard had taken so many drugs that he barely breathed when he was awake, and she wasn't sure he breathed at all when he was sleeping. Howard's chest never moved, but the mirror would slowly cloud and Donna would cry.

Then she would pick up her pillow with both hands and hold it just above his face. Who would know? Who would care? Donna stood there, for hours, praying for the strength to free them both, but it never came. Always, the next morning, the monster came back to life.

That is how Donna came to think of her gladiator: He was a monster, all the more frightening because he still looked so much like the man she loved. But Donna could tell the difference. This monster's face was puffed up and pushed around, like a fighter's, like a losing fighter's. Howard had been fighting himself, and losing, for a long time.

There were times when he still sounded like the man she loved but never for long because he had forgotten how.

"I love you," Howard said, and he brought her flowers, but Donna threw them at him. "You can't buy me with flowers," Donna said. "I want my husband back."

"I love you," he said, and he brought her diamond bracelets and diamond rings, but Donna threw them at him. "You can't buy me with diamonds," she said. "I want my husband back."

"I love you," Howard said, and he bought her a sailboat as big as their house. Howard bought Donna a 32-foot sailboat, but she wouldn't look at it. "You can't buy me with sailboats," she said. "I want my husband back."

Howard did not understand this. The other women were happy with flowers and jewels and cocaine. The other women were happy just to go to parties on sailboats and take their tops off and drink champagne. What was the matter with his wife?

Howard did not ask politely. Howard raged, all of a sudden, for no reason that Donna could see or sense. But Donna couldn't see the little men or the electricity shooting from the walls. Howard would suddenly jump up and start calling at her, calling her names, tearing her down. Howard had become Roger, without a gun, but Howard did not need a gun to wound Donna and he did not need a gun to kill her.

One day, as he screamed at her and she screamed at him, Howard ran out of the house and jumped in his car. Donna ran after him, and he turned the car toward her. Howard aimed his Eldorado at his wife and gunned the gas. Donna jumped aside in time, but Howard never slowed down.

When Howard left, Donna prayed. Howard came back smiling and carrying two bags of hamburgers from MacDonald's, as though nothing had happened.

This is what was so hard for Donna, bobbing blindly on Howard's waves. She never knew when he would lift her, gentle and warm, and when he would turn violent and cold and try to drag her under. The gentle Howard always apologized for being angry, when he remembered being angry, and told Donna he never meant to hurt her. Howard said it, and then he hurt her again. And always, Donna told him: "I don't want apologies. I want you to stop using drugs."

Sick and crazy and angry as he was, Howard tried again to quit, because he had already tried everything else. He tried leaving Donna, but he was miserable. She tried leaving him, but he always begged her to come back. He knew he could survive for a little while in a penthouse with women and cocaine, but he could not survive for long. Even as he made her feel so small and helpless, Howard loved Donna enough to try living sober.

Each time he tried, it got harder and he kept trying to do it the wrong way. Howard would not go to a clinic or a doctor or a hospital, because he would not admit that he needed to. He had done that once, and it didn't work. That was Howard's excuse: It didn't work. He would not admit that he never gave it a chance—that he went there to hide, not to get well. Howard knew he was a drug addict, but he would not face it and no one could make him.

Howard's mind and soul and spirit all failed him, but not his ego. As low as he fell, Howard still wanted to believe he could do anything he tried. He could play baseball, he could overturn laws and he could quit drugs.

So Donna locked him in the house every weekend, just as Judy used to lock him in the office, and Howard went to battle with his demons. Every Friday afternoon, Donna went through the house with Howard and threw out every pill and joint and cocaine rock he had hidden through the week. Donna flushed his cocaine down the toilet, and Howard felt good. Howard always felt good Friday nights, when his mind and body were still running on the drugs he had taken all week. Friday nights, Howard was full of promise and hope, and Donna wanted to believe they were in love again.

She still wanted to believe by Saturday, when Howard was sweating and swearing and hollering at the walls, and she still wanted to believe by Sunday, when he was vomiting and choking and doubled over in pain. Donna wanted to believe on Monday, but she knew better. Donna would follow Howard to work, to make sure he didn't stop along the way.

Howard didn't have to. Howard never had to drive down alleys to meet thugs who carried guns. Howard bought his drugs in the courthouse or in offices near the courthouse or in coffee shops where judges and lawyers always met the people who sold them whatever they wanted. By lunchtime Monday, Howard had his pills and pot and crack cocaine. Howard was in the worst business for a man who was trying to stay away from drugs.

Donna loved him for trying, as much as she hated him for failing, and she tried to understand what made him so sick. Donna started going to meetings for drug addicts and families of drug addicts. There were plenty to choose from, listed in the papers with garage sales and puppet shows. Donna learned a lot at those meetings. She learned that she was not alone. She learned that all addicts manipulate the people around them, and that those people come to need feeling needed. She learned that it was natural to love and hate her monster, and that he needed to tear her down because he had lost all of his own self respect. But Donna still refused to learn the most important lesson of all: That whether Howard got well was up to him, and there was nothing she could do. Howard would have to hit bottom, by himself, even if it killed him.

Donna went to meetings and she prayed. Howard went to work and took drugs, but he stopped bringing them home. Howard could not quit, but he saw how much Donna wanted to believe he could, and he wanted her to believe it. Howard tried with all his might to stay away from crack, and he took his other drugs at work, even if he had to work late. He hid the pills that he needed to get through the nights and weekends, and he made Donna believe, just as he made juries believe.

She believed enough to get pregnant. Donna had told Howard to forget about having children until he was done with drugs, but Howard swore he had been clean for months. Howard and Donna flew to Lake Tahoe in February 1987 to ski and to celebrate. The celebration ended in a restaurant, in the middle of dinner with friends. Howard went to the men's room, and when he came back to the table, Donna saw the white powder on his upper lip.

The lake road back to the hotel was high and icy, with a

sharp drop to the side. Donna drove fast and reckless, and she screamed at Howard the whole way.

"You think we're going to die?" she shouted. "I want to fucking die. I want you to fucking die."

The next day, Donna flew to San Francisco, and Howard called. He was coming to join her, to apologize. Donna drove to the airport to pick him up. Howard walked off the plane raving.

"Fuck you," he said. "Who are you to run out on me to stay with your dyke friends. You must be a fucking dyke."

Donna did not talk back to Howard, but she talked to herself. Stay centered. Don't get dragged into an argument that doesn't make sense. Leave him alone.

The less Donna said, the angrier Howard got. Howard jumped on a chair and started pulling garbage from the waste can. He threw garbage at Donna in the airport.

"I don't need your help," he said. "You need help."

Donna finally answered him.

"Howard," she said, "grow up."

"I don't have to grow up," he said. "You have to grow down. You're an old woman."

Then Howard ran out of garbage and he threw his suitcases, and the police came and told them both to leave. Donna drove Howard to her friend's apartment. When they got there, Howard looked just the way he did when he came back with the MacDonald's hamburgers after he tried to run her over. Howard looked as though nothing had happened.

For a long time, most of the time they knew each other, Donna took Howard's insults personally. For a long time, Donna blamed herself. If she were smarter and tougher and stronger, she thought, she could solve his problems and her problems, once and for all, but she was a failure who couldn't even kill herself and didn't have the guts to kill Howard. All that time, she kept throwing out Howard's drugs and locking him in the house and screaming back when he screamed at her, but she was done with that now because she knew better. Donna knew it wasn't her fault.

Donna knew it wasn't her fault, but that did not solve

Howard's problem or hers. She still sat in her house all day, smoking cigarettes and eating and crying while she waited for the monster to come home. When he did, she begged him to try harder, and she begged harder than she had ever begged in her life. She begged Howard to give her a chance, and to give their baby a chance and to give himself a chance. She begged him to go to a marriage counselor, and he did, and he told the counselor it was all Donna's fault. She begged him to go to meetings or go to a doctor or go to another clinic. She begged him to remember the time when he believed he could be anything in the world, except selfish.

Donna begged. Howard smoked cocaine.

She stopped going to the office and she stopped going anywhere. She could not bear to have more people ask what was the matter, and then tell her she was wrong, or crazy. There was only one person who did not tell her that, the only other person who loved Howard enough to throw him out. Howard had never fooled his mother.

Charlotte Finkelstein had remarried and did not live far from her son. They talked now, and Howard was glad, but he didn't want her advice any more than he wanted it when he was in high school. She saved it for Donna. Howard's mother told Donna to stop trying to save her son and start trying to save herself.

"Get out of the house," she said. "Get dressed and get out. Get a job. Do anything to keep him from pulling you down with him."

Donna listened, again and again, and thought about it while she thought about her baby. The more she listened, the more it made sense. She could not give up on herself, not with the baby coming, but she could give up on Howard if it was the only way to save herself and her child. Donna started to go out of the house and started to understand again that she was a real person, not Howard's pet. Donna called a friend who owned a travel agency and asked for lessons on the computer. When she knew enough about ordering tickets to pretend she had experience, she looked through the want ads and applied for a job.

Pregnant and 34 years old, Donna went to work in a travel agency and prepared to leave her husband. She had to stay until she gave birth, because she needed his insurance, but by then she would have enough money and confidence to move out. From the day she started working, Howard's words hurt her less and less. He could call her worthless and lazy and stupid and anything else, but she knew better. Donna finally released herself in her own care, not Howard's.

The only way Howard could hurt Donna was to hurt himself, and he hurt himself more than ever. Howard fumbled from pill to pill, looking for new drugs to numb his aches. He liked Dilaudid because it made him even number than Percodan did and it would have made him number still if he had listened to Debbie. Debbie was a client and she was as crazy as Roger, although Howard couldn't see that. Debbie sold him Dilaudid and laughed at the way he swallowed it. "Every good junkie knows you shoot Dilaudid," she said. "Break it down and shoot it into your arms, Howard. Don't be such a sissy."

Howard didn't think he was a sissy, but he didn't like the idea of needles. He was afraid of them and he didn't need to be any more afraid than he already was. Howard took Debbie's Dilaudid and swallowed it, until the police took Debbie's Dilaudid away. The detectives came in May and took 400 pills and all her needles and they wanted to know: "Who buys this from you?" Debbie wouldn't tell them, but she told Howard this: "You'd better find a way to get them back and get me off, or else."

Howard said he would, but he was more afraid of Donna. Donna did not tell him she was going to leave, but Howard could feel it, even through the drugs, because she wasn't scared of him any more. Now it was Howard's turn to beg, and he did. He promised, again, that he would try to quit, and Donna listened, although she didn't believe it. Howard tried to quit again, every weekend, and failed again, every time. What if they could make the weekend last, long enough to give his mind and body a chance, far enough from South Florida to keep Howard from running to his old friends for help?

It was the end of May when they went to Aruba, where Howard was supposed to get well and prove that he could stay that way. Howard failed again, because it wasn't a matter of will. Howard failed because he was too sick to make himself better, although he still wouldn't admit it. Howard had to choose between his ego and his life. His ego won. Donna knew there was no point in trying to hold him up any longer, and she let go, to save herself. Donna knew she would not have to leave him, because she was certain that Howard was going to die.

In June, after they came back from Aruba, Donna took out a $250,000 life insurance policy on her monster and started to plan her life as a widow.

For the first time since she knew him, Howard stopped fighting, because he knew he lost. For six weeks, Howard did not fight and he did not pretend. He got up in the morning, or in the afternoon, and he took his pills and smoked his crack and drove his Cadillac. Donna prayed only that Howard killed himself before he killed anyone else, but she didn't try to stop him. Donna let go, to save herself and her child, and waited for someone to call and tell her Howard was dead.

The phone rang just after midnight, Friday, July 2, 1987.

A jury that won't listen

Howard could barely see them, but he could feel them. Howard could feel his whole life pressing down on his chest before he began, slowly, to make out the faces. He knew these people, and they all knew him, too well.

Howard could see his father, and his mother. Howard could see his brother Ricky. He could see his partner, Ron. One by one, the faces became clearer, but Howard did not want to see them. Howard had faced this jury before, every day of his life, but he wasn't ready for them now, even though he was the only one who got any sleep the night before.

When Howard called from jail after he hit the police car, Donna called everyone they knew with the good news: "Howard is not dead." They had all let go of him, as they had to, and Howard fell hard, as he had to. But he lived, as they hadn't dared to hope. Now they had to pick him up. They talked all night about how to do it.

Wayne Spath called Frank Foltz at five minutes after four in the morning. Wayne was a bondsman as well as a friend, and he was ready to post $3,500 to bail Howard out of jail. Frank was a drug counselor, and he was ready to argue Howard into treatment. He knew Howard had tried before, and he knew why Howard failed. This time, Howard had to understand and give in. When they got to the jail at 7:30 Saturday morning, Howard couldn't understand a thing.

Nearly a half-day after his arrest, Howard still couldn't stand on his own. The jailers wouldn't release him, for his own good. So the bondsman and the drug counselor went out for breakfast and came back and waited for a couple of hours in the hallway, until Howard could wobble to the car. They drove only a few blocks, to Howard's office, where his family and friends were waiting. That was Frank's idea. He specialized in intervention, in forcing a drug addict to confront his habit and get help. The best way, Frank said, was to force Howard to confront the people who cared about him, the people he used and hurt. If there was anything left of the Howard Finkelstein who loved them, there was a chance he would hear and he would want to be healed.

Howard heard, but he could not make out what they were saying. He saw their faces, but he saw them as his jury, not his friends. The only part of Howard that could do anything but sit in his fat, leather chair and stare across the wide, teak desk and wonder what was happening was the lawyer part, and Howard the lawyer could not just sit there. Howard the lawyer began to argue as soon as he could make words come out of his mouth.

"I was trapped," Howard said. "I was fooled by the cops, by whoever gave me those drugs. I've made a lot of enemies, and you know that. I've made enemies because I care about the poor and the powerless. There are a lot of people who would rather not have me around any more, and you can't let them win. If you care about me and the people I believe in, you have to stand by me. Don't let them take me away."

All the while Howard talked, he fumbled through the desk drawers and poked his head underneath and got up and stumbled around the room, as though he were looking for something very important, because he was. Howard found his spare briefcase, and as he opened the latch it slipped, and his papers and pens spilled onto his desk. But he couldn't find any pills. So while they all kept talking, Howard picked up his telephone and dialed. "I need to see you," he said, and that was all. The woman he called understood.

A few minutes later, there was a knock at the door. Howard was already there, waiting. A man handed him pills and Howard pushed them into his mouth before anyone realized what he had done, and when they did, they all gasped and jumped up, but Frank told them to sit down. Let him go, Frank said. He doesn't know yet that he has hit bottom.

Howard didn't know anything, except that he suddenly felt stronger. What had they done to him last night? He had never been so confused, so weak. Someone gave him something, someone who wanted to hurt him, but he survived and now he was stronger. Now that he had his own drugs, he would win over this jury, as he always did.

But this jury was not a fair jury. This jury argued back, and shouted at him and called him names. This jury called him a liar.

Howard let them talk, but he did not listen. Howard never listened to anyone but Howard and he expected everyone else to do the same. When they were done, Howard started again, and he did not stop. He blamed everyone but himself. He told them, all of them, that they failed him and they failed themselves, and that they were being used. Howard kept talking, for hours, until they were all exhausted and Howard believed he had won. Howard thought he was going to walk out a free man, until Frank held his hand up in mid-sentence and looked him in the eye.

"Howard," he said, "you are a pain in the ass. You are going into treatment whether you like it or not."

Howard didn't have a chance to argue. His brother Ricky tackled him. They carried him out to the parking lot and stuffed him backward into a car and drove him to Ricky's house. Howard screamed and kicked all the way. "You sold me out," he shouted. "You are a goddam terrorist." When they got Howard inside, he spun around and ran straight at his brother. Howard tried to run through Ricky. Howard tried it again and again. Finally, Ricky grabbed Howard by the shoulders and pushed him hard against the wall.

"Shut up," he said, "and don't fight this." Then, when Maury arrived, Ricky took the cranks off the windows and the knobs off the doors and locked Howard in the bedroom. "Try to get some sleep," they told him, but Howard didn't want to sleep.

Howard wanted cocaine. Howard picked up the phone and called his friends until he found one willing to make a delivery.

Ricky was not surprised to see the drug dealer when he answered the door, but he was surprised that Howard had been so stupid. Ricky and Maury let Howard thrash and scream all day, but they didn't let him have any more drugs. It was night before Howard finally fell asleep, for a little while, and then he woke up, calling for Donna.

"Get Donna," he said. "I have to talk to Donna. I have to find out if Donna is all right."

Howard had not seen Donna on the jury at his office because Donna did not want to be there. Donna sat in the next room, waiting, drinking coffee, until late afternoon, until the pain began. Donna thought she was having her baby, or losing her baby, and she was rushed to the hospital while Howard argued with his jury.

Now Howard woke up and remembered, and he was worried. Ricky brought the phone and dialed the hospital, and when Donna came on the line he handed the phone to Howard.

"Thanks," Howard said, and then he put his hand over the mouthpiece and asked a question: "Who is this woman and what is she calling about?"

Howard passed out again, and the next time he woke up he started eating and he didn't stop. He couldn't stop eating and he couldn't stop talking. Howard was arguing again, with everyone. "I'm all right," he said. "Look at me. I'm fine now. I don't need to go anywhere except home. I need to get some rest so that I can get back to work. I have to be in court."

Maury looked at his son and realized that Howard didn't understand what had happened.

"Howard," he said, "you don't have any work to do and I don't know if you will ever have any work to do. You were arrested, and you'll probably lose your license. You might not ever be a lawyer again. If you don't let us help you, you're going to go back to jail. "

Going to jail? Howard thought about that, and he thought he might as well if he couldn't be a lawyer. How could Howard not be a lawyer? How could Howard be anything but a lawyer? For a long time now, Howard thought he would die, but this was worse. He never thought about living and not being a lawyer. Howard stopped fighting and he stopped arguing. Howard said he would do anything his father wanted, and he went back to the refrigerator. He opened the door, reached in and fell asleep.

The family drove to Boca Raton the next morning, the Fourth of July. Howard's brothers and sisters were all there when Howard arrived at the drug treatment center. When the car pulled up to the red-brick, circular drive, Howard thought Maury made a wrong turn. This is a restaurant, he thought, or it is a hotel.

If it was a drug clinic, it was even nicer than the last one. The carpet was soft, the pastel walls soothing. There was an Olympic pool and tennis courts and a weight room and an elegant dining room with a ceiling so high it hurt Howard's neck to look up at it. There were waiters, too, and they brought as many servings as a guest could want. "This is not so bad," Howard thought. "I can spend a few weeks here, and make everyone happy."

For the first time in a very long time, Howard and his family agreed. "This is a beautiful place," they all thought. "Howard can do this." They helped Howard settle into a room about the size of a room in a good hotel, with an earth-tone carpet and two single beds and a desk and a picture window that framed a man-made lake. Except for Howard's 300-pound roommate, everything they saw was perfect.

That is what families were supposed to see. This was no field hospital for the victims of South Florida's drug war. This was a drive-in theater where husbands and wives and parents could park their Volvos and Lincolns for a little while and see how that war was being won, even if it wasn't. They did not see the therapy wards beyond the picture windows and pastel walls, and they did not hear the screams.

Howard heard them, all that night, and he joined the chorus of men and women wailing for their lost souls.

This time, Howard gagged and puked and screamed through the easy part of quitting. This time, while Howard's mind struggled with cocaine, his body struggled with all those pills. He felt his bones burst through his skin and burn in the open air. Howard felt as though his body were trying to turn itself inside out, to escape from itself. Howard's body convulsed while his mind shouted for more cocaine. It was Wednesday before Howard's shouting and screaming and puking were done and his mind began to the clear. It was Wednesday when Howard began to realize how desperate he really was.

He knew something horrible happened, but he couldn't remember. He could not remember the crash or where he was that night or which night it was. He remembered waking up in jail and he remembered being in his office with all those people. What was that about? Then he remembered what his father said: "You might not be a lawyer again."

Howard began to shake. This was worse than the last time he went to the clinic. This was worse than all those times Donna flushed his cocaine down the toilet. This was worse than having little men talking all night and electricity shooting out of walls. This was worse, because Howard could not run away and hide and he couldn't tell his father and his wife to chase the bad people away. This was worse, because Howard finally had to face his demons, alone. He had no idea how to do it.

When Donna and Frank and Maury came to visit, Howard told them all the same thing. "I have to get out of here. I have to straighten this out with the court and the Bar. I have to take care of my case."

"Don't worry about your case," they said, "because there's nothing you can do." Howard could not represent himself and win. He needed a lawyer who had no connection to his clients or his lies or his drugs. Howard knew that, and he hated it.

All those years, Howard fought the legal system and now he was at its mercy. All those years, Howard fought to keep from becoming a lawyer who cared more about money than justice, and he lost, and now he needed to find a lawyer who cared about him. Howard thought that would be harder than quitting cocaine, but it wasn't.

Ever since Howard's arrest, since the corpse photo appeared in the papers, friends had been calling to offer help. A lot of his friends were lawyers, and a lot of them knew other lawyers. This is all politics, a lot of them said. Howard will be the victim of politics unless he hires a lawyer with the right connections. The same names came up, again and again. But one name stood out, not only because he was good, but because he was sincere. One of the best criminal lawyers in South Florida wanted to help Howard because he believed in Howard. He wanted Howard to keep practicing law because he believed in Howard's kind of law. He believed ever since he was a young judge and Howard was a young public defender who persuaded him to throw out a law against sleeping on the beach.

Howard could not believe how lucky he was that Harry Gulkin wanted to defend him.

Howard trusted Harry, and so did Donna. When Donna first talked to Harry about Howard's case, they discovered a funny thing. They both came from the same part of New Jersey. Harry even knew a family named Chase, years before, when he represented a pharmacist from West Orange who lost his business. It was Donna's father. She was sure then that Harry was meant to help Howard, too.

When Howard heard Harry wanted to represent him, he began to believe that he would survive.

Learning to live

Howard's first days in treatment were painful but easy. All he did was vomit and argue, and Howard was practiced at both.

The counselors told him what counselors had told him before, what he already knew: "You are a drug addict, and you always will be a drug addict." Why did they keep saying it?

Howard did not think he needed convincing. He already agreed to be cured, so why not just go ahead with it? Whatever it was, whatever they wanted to do, let them do it and be done. Howard trusted Harry to make a deal with the court, and he trusted himself to make a deal with the therapists, as soon as he figured out what they really wanted.

"We want you to surrender," the therapists said. "You must surrender to a force greater than yourself. You have to make a list of all your mistakes, and all the people you hurt, and you have to make amends. You have to go to those people and apologize. You have to stand up in front of complete strangers and admit those mistakes, and admit you are an addict. You have to ask God for help."

Howard listened, but he was too smart to fall for it. Why should he surrender? Did they think he had a gun? Did they think he was some street-corner crackhead with a gun, hiding in a burned-out house? "Listen," Howard said. "I just want to get this over with."

"You listen," the therapist said. "Listen to yourself. If I went into a cancer ward, or an AIDS ward, and I said I had a cure, everyone would want to know what it was. But not drug addicts. A drug addict just wants to make a deal to keep being a drug addict."

Howard listened, and he nodded, but he did not get the point at all. Howard could not see what the fuss was all about, because he could not see himself. Howard had not seen himself for many years, since he closed his eyes.

It was the second week in treatment when Howard's eyes began to open, when the cocaine and Percodan and Dilaudid finally drained from his blood and mind. When Howard's eyes began to open, he began to shake and vomit all over again, and there was nothing left to argue about.

Howard's eyes began to open when Harry came. Harry came or called every day with news from court, and every day the news was worse.

When Howard's eyes were closed, it all seemed simple: Harry would make a deal and Howard would enter a plea and he would apologize to the court and the Bar and all would be forgiven. By the second week, Howard began to understand that forgiveness was not so easy.

Instead of reducing the charges, the prosecutors wanted to increase them. They wanted to charge Howard with trafficking, with being a dealer, and they could do it because he was carrying so many pills in his briefcase. A trafficking conviction would mean at least 10 years in prison. Howard would lose his license for at least three years no matter how the court case turned out.

Howard shook and Howard vomited and Howard begged Harry to explain: "Why are they doing this to me?"

"Because," Harry said, "they think you are a liar. They think you lied to a judge about a drug dealer named Debbie."

Howard could not make sense of it. All he could remember was this: The morning of the day he crashed into the police car, Howard went to court and persuaded a judge to release Debbie's drugs. That afternoon, he took them to Debbie's house, but he couldn't remember anything after that. He couldn't remember how he got to the street in Lauderhill, and he couldn't remember the crash.

"What does Debbie have to do with this?" he asked.

Harry explained that a few days after Howard's arrest, the detective who raided Debbie's house complained to the judge. The detective said he told Howard the drugs couldn't be released because the police were still investigating, but Howard never told that to the judge and the hearing was held when the detective was out of town. Worst of all, some of the pills found in Howard's car were Debbie's. It looked as though Howard lied to the judge to get drugs for himself, and it looked as though Howard and Debbie might be in business together.

"Goddam," Howard said. "These are all lies, and we can prove it. I'm going to fight and I'm going to win. No jury is going to believe this crap."

Harry did not argue with Howard. Harry reached into his jacket pocket and took out a photograph. It looked like the photograph of a dead man. It was Howard's booking mug.

"Look at this," Harry said. "This is what the jury will see. Do you really think a jury will believe this man?"

Howard could not look at the picture, and he could not look away. The drugs were gone from Howard's body, at last, but he felt worse than ever because he could not hide from what he had become. The more Howard understood about his life, about his awful and confused and hurtful life, the less he wanted to live.

"Bad as it all seems," Harry said, "you still have a chance to save yourself and your license and to be a husband again, and a father. You need to get well. You need to do everything you can to stay clean and you need to show the court and the Bar and the world that you won't ever go back. If you do all that, if you stop fighting, there is a chance."

Howard thought about that chance, but it already seemed too small, too far away. Now that his eyes were open, he could see all the people he lied to, and the people he hurt. Howard could see Donna, and he could see himself without her. Howard could see himself driving blind, and he could see that he could have killed someone before he killed himself. Howard could not bear to see any of it.

He thought about running away, and he thought about killing himself, but he had seen Andy run away and he had seen Donna try to kill herself. Howard could not run and he could not die, but he did not know how to live with the man he had become. Howard panicked, and the panic lasted for days, until he was exhausted, until he finally surrendered.

Two weeks after he crashed into the police car, Howard walked down the hall to see his therapist and he said: "Please, teach me how to live. I want to live, but I don't know how. Tell me how to live."

The therapist told him, right away, and Howard tried to understand. "You can never pick up a drug or a drink again," the therapist said, and Howard agreed. Howard could understand that, and he wanted to believe he could do it.

Then the therapist told him the rest: "You must change everything."

Howard was not sure what he meant, but he meant what he said. Howard had to change everything in his life. He had to change his friends and his job, and he had to spend his time in different places. Howard thought about it, and he agreed. He would change everything, so he could live.

He told the therapist he would change everything but this: "I will not cut my hair."

Now it was the therapist who did not understand. "You have to cut your hair to surrender," he said.

"I will surrender myself," Howard said, "but I will not surrender my beliefs."

The next two weeks were not as painful, because Howard was busier. Howard was busy recovering, and planning his new life. Howard threw himself into the recovery program the way he had thrown himself into every cause he ever believed in, completely and with all his might. Howard went to therapy sessions and meetings with other addicts. He began to exercise again, to build his strength. The day Howard surrendered, Donna could hear it in his voice and she could see it in his eyes. She knew that Howard could see now, and that he finally saw himself, and that he finally saw beyond himself.

"He has opened the black curtain," she thought, and she believed he would be well.

Donna was recovering too, and working as hard as Howard. She went through a program for codependents. The therapists helped sort through her feelings about the man she loved and hated, the man who brought her flowers and diamonds and tried to run her over with his Cadillac. Donna was not alone in her anger. Like everyone in the group, Donna wrote down everything her addict had done to make her angry, and she tied the list to a balloon. As the weeks went on, all the rest released their balloons and released their anger, but Donna couldn't.

Donna waited until the end to let go.

The treatment center released Howard after four weeks, on his 34th birthday, but he did not go home because he was not ready to be home. Howard agreed to spend the next month in a halfway house near the court, where he could begin to make amends.

There was no red-brick driveway at the St. Francis Mission. There was no swimming pool or tennis court or weight room. There was just an old, low, stucco plug of a building that leaned back from the street and got all tangled in wild vines and dry trees, and there was Pastor Conny, grown-up tough kid and former police chaplain.

Howard shared a small room with three other men: a killer, a drug dealer and a homosexual professor. There were no waiters to bring him dinner. Howard cooked, and Howard washed the dishes. He began the day the way everyone else did, with meditation, at quarter to eight in the morning. Pastor Conny did not ask anyone to join his Lutheran prayers, or any prayers, but he made them take time to sit in the cool, dark chapel and think. He knew they would think about God.

Howard walked the narrow hallways and sat under the trees and lay on his bed. He listened to the Gregorian chants that echoed from the loudspeakers, and even Howard began to think about God.

Every day, Howard walked out of the mission and down the street to his office to settle affairs. Howard could not drive because the police took his license and they took his car. As he walked down the street, he walked past the people who used to crowd the courtrooms to watch the big-time lawyer, and Howard knew they were watching him now, for a different reason.

One last lesson

The old man's feet disappeared. Howard followed him from the car to the beach, watching his thin, white legs wrestle with the earth, but those were not feet that sank in the hot sand. Those were not feet of flesh or clay.

Those were grapefruits, or melons.

Howard watched the old man pull these fat, pale melons from the sand and push them in again, one by one. Howard watched him stop to rest every few steps, and Howard listened to the old man's lungs crying for him to stop for good. Howard wanted to help, but the old man didn't want Howard's help. He wanted Howard to follow.

Howard followed Andy Mavrides for the last time.

Halfway down to the sea, Andy sat in the sand and Howard sat in the sand, and Howard listened while Andy talked. The teacher had learned too late for himself, but not too late to teach Howard. Andy had come back to surrender, and to make amends. He surrendered to the courts, and the Bar, and he started to work as a clerk, to pay back his debts. Andy wanted to be a lawyer again, the kind of lawyer he should have been all along, but it was too late. While Howard was in the treatment center, Andy was in the hospital. The doctors told him he had cancer, and he was dying. He was 56 years old.

"I made a lot of mistakes," Andy said, "but one was bigger and worse than all the rest. I ran away. Don't run away, Howard. Don't let them take your license. Do whatever the doctor tells you and whatever the judge tells you and whatever the Bar tells you. Do whatever you have to do to be a lawyer again."

Howard promised he would, and he did. Howard pleaded guilty Aug. 26, 1987.

Harry Gulkin made the best deal he could, probably the best deal anybody could. The prosecutors traded the trafficking charge for the guilty plea, but they were not willing to drop the rest. They wanted Howard convicted of felonies, and that could be enough to ruin his career. They were willing to recommend probation, but that would not keep Howard out of jail if the judge thought he belonged there.

Howard could not wait to find out, but he had no choice. The judge would not rule for three months, until she was sure about him. Howard would be investigated before he was sentenced, and there was no place to hide.

The reporters were waiting when Howard walked out of the courtroom. Harry and Donna took Howard's arms and started to lead him away, but Howard stopped. "I can't be a hypocrite," he said. "I always talked to them before, and I'll talk to them now."

"I've been sick," Howard said, "but I'm getting well and I want another chance." The reporters asked him if he wanted to admit that he was wrong about drugs.

"Do you still think they should be legal?"

"Yes," Howard said. "I do. I'm a drug addict, but that's my problem. It isn't the drugs that are evil. The evil is within me."

For the next three months, people Howard didn't know poked their noses into his most private and shameful business. For three months, Howard peed in a bottle to prove he was sober, while his doctors and counselors and friends told strangers everything they knew about him. For three months, the ponytailed gladiator who never worried about the future worried about nothing else. Nothing, not cocaine or Roger or the thought of losing Donna, ever made him more afraid.

For a little while, when he first surrendered, Howard didn't have to think about it, because he was busy. For a little while, when he lived in the church, Howard filled his mind with chants and prayers and he believed that one day he would wake up and this would all be over.

But when Howard went home, and he was alone, Howard stopped being busy and he stopped chanting and he stopped dreaming and he wondered: "What next? What happens next?" And then the fear rushed up from behind and knocked him over.

What next? Howard had never thought of such a thing before. He had been busy with drugs for nearly 20 years, and he had been dreaming all that time. Howard stopped looking where he was going when he was 16 years old, and now, all of a sudden, he had to find his way. Howard not only had to find his way through life, he had to find his way through the day, through the next hour.

What next? Howard did not know, and he had to find out for himself. Recovering from drug addiction was not at all like recovering from the flu or from cancer or from a broken leg. There was no medicine to take, no radiation, no surgery, no follow-up visits to the doctor. There was nothing to do at all except go to meetings every night, and those lasted only an hour or two. Howard had to find his way through each day, and nothing around him looked familiar at all.

Howard had never seen the adult world without drugs. He never watched a movie, he never had sex, he never went to sleep without drugs. He never got angry and he never laughed. He did not know how to do any of it sober, and he could not ask his friends for help.

Howard could not join the other lawyers in the bars after work, and he could not call his old drug pals. Donna tried to help, but she had to care for her mother, and she was about to have a baby. Howard paced through the house. Then he cleaned the house, and then he paced again. Howard finally took up golf to pass the time.

Every day, Howard went to the golf course and practiced on the driving range for an hour, and then he played 18 holes. Howard played with recovering addicts he met at the meetings, and he played with his brother and he played with strangers. Howard played golf and he carried his fear along with his clubs, while he waited to find out: What next?

Howard carried his fear into the courtroom when he was called to answer for Debbie's drugs. A month after he pleaded guilty to possession, expecting probation, Howard stood before a different judge, who could send him to jail. This judge made no deal. This judge held a warrant charging Howard with contempt of court, and he wanted to know why Howard asked him to release Debbie's drugs after the police turned him down. The judge said Howard led him to believe the police approved.

He looked down at Howard, over the top of his glasses, and asked him: "Did you lie to me?"

Howard answered quietly, but without hesitation: "No, I did not lie, and I did not mean to mislead you, but I know I did. I did not speak clearly then, but I can speak clearly now, and I can think clearly. I want you to know I'm sorry, sincerely sorry."

The judge looked and listened, and finally spoke: "I don't know if you lied, and I am not going to ruin you because of something I don't know. I know you have problems, and I know you can solve them. Solve your problems, Howard. You have too much to offer to waste your life."

Howard thanked the judge, and he meant it, but he was no less afraid. He dragged his fear out of the courtroom and went home to wait for his sentence.

While he waited, his court file grew fat with letters. They were all good, and some were remarkable. It wasn't just that lawyers stood up for him, lawyers who also stood up for drug dealers and killers. Howard's clients stood up for him, the clients no one else cared about. Secretaries and clerks and old schoolmates stood up for him, because he had always been kind to them.

Even prosecutors stood up for him, people he fought and beat, because he beat them fair and decent. Even a police chief stood up for Howard; even a supervisor of narcotics detectives from the department that arrested him.

Howard read the letters, and they overwhelmed him, but they did not take away his fear. Howard read the letters and thought he didn't deserve any of it. Howard pleaded guilty, and he felt guilty. He felt more guilty about hurting his friends and his family than about hurting himself. He felt guilty because the letters reminded him of all he had done for other people, and all that he might never do again, because he had been selfish. Howard read the letters and hugged his fear and cried for hours, and he went to sleep exhausted every night.

Donna woke him up at 1 a.m. Oct. 16, and Howard felt the greatest fear of all. He was about to become a father. Between court hearings and addiction meetings and therapy sessions, Howard and Donna had been going to birth classes so that Howard could coach her through delivery, without drugs. And all the while, Donna was coaching Howard, who worried about her and about the baby and, most of all, whether he could be the husband and father they deserved. Donna poked him awake and told him it was time.

Saria Michele was born at 4 a.m. It was the most important moment of Howard's life.

When Howard was young, he was so sure he knew everything, and when Howard was older, he was so sure he knew nothing. But when he saw Saria, he knew, at last, what was important. Howard knew, all at once, the difference between the mind and the spirit, and he knew it was the spirit that connected him to that child and that woman. It was the spirit that connected them all to this earth.

Howard dropped his fear and he picked up his daughter.

Howard was not afraid when he walked with Harry and Donna into courtroom 416 on Nov. 18, 1987. When the sentencing hearing began, at 9:30 a.m., the courtroom was full. So was the hallway. The men and women who had come so many times to watch the Howard show and who had come to admire and respect Howard now came, shoulder to shoulder, to show the judge how they felt.

Harry brought nine witnesses to speak about Howard's

character. Five of them were judges. Two were prosecutors. The eighth was Frank Foltz, who was appointed by the court to monitor Howard's progress. The last was Al Schreiber, Howard's first boss and still the public defender.

The judges and the prosecutors and the public defender all said the same, that in all the years Howard had been arguing for his clients and his beliefs, he had argued well and with passion. If he was a drug addict, he was no less a lawyer, no less an advocate. The courts would be poorer without him.

Foltz brought word from the doctors and counselors, and the lab reports: Howard showed a deep commitment to recovery. He was clean, and he showed every sign of staying clean.

Harry told the judge how he felt about Howard, not just as a client, but as a man and a lawyer, and then he called one more witness: Howard. He did not bring a bag of sex toys or a dead man's shirt or a table with a bloody hand print. Howard looked up at Judge Patti Englander Henning and just told the truth.

First he told her how thankful he was just to be standing there.

"There's no doubt in my mind that if I had continued the way I was going, death was inevitable," he said. "In fact, I reached such utter despair that death not only was acceptable, at certain times it was desirable."

Then he went on:

"What happened to me was my own doing," he said. "I can't blame anyone else. It was one thing for me to suffer, but it's another to hurt the people who loved me, to make them watch me disintegrate as a human being. I have gone into treatment and I walked in on my knees. I needed to learn a new way to live. I did not know how to live anymore. I learned that the only way to live was to surrender. I chose to live, and I am a very lucky man. I came out of this with my life, with my wife and now with a child. I will forever carry the burden of what I did to my family. I know that. I accept it. I ask this court to find compassion and mercy. If I get the chance, I will work harder, more diligently and with more honor than I ever have in my life."

Howard got the chance. The judge told him he would get no

special treatment for all the letters and testimony from important people. He would be treated for what he was, a sick man who had never been charged with a crime before. She did not find him guilty of any charges except driving under the influence, but she did not set him free.

The judge fined Howard $2,000, put him on probation for five years, and ordered him to donate 100 hours of his time to a good cause every year of his probation. She also suspended his driver's license, ordered him to stay in a drug treatment program for two years and give urine or blood samples without warning.

In a sense, the judge left the question of Howard's guilt up to Howard. She withheld ruling on the drug charges until his probation was done, one way or the other. If he stayed clean, he stayed innocent. If he failed, even once, he would be a convicted felon. He still did not know if he would be a lawyer.

Technically, he still was, but there was nothing for him to do. The Florida Bar waits until a criminal case against a lawyer is over before making a recommendation to the state Supreme Court. In Howard's case, the rules called for a minimum suspension of three years. For the maximum, he could be disbarred. He had to wait again to find out, but Howard did not hide under a blanket or behind his fears.

Howard volunteered to enter a program to help lawyers with addictions. He had a lot of company. Howard had always known other lawyers who took drugs, the lawyers who invited him into the bathrooms at parties, but he did not know there were so many. The Bar could not throw them all out, but it threw out the ones who would not admit their problems and who would not get help. Howard admitted it, and he did whatever he was asked.

While he waited for the Bar's decision, he finished the last of his work and left his private office for good. Howard stopped pretending to be a lawyer, even before he had to, and walked back to the courthouse, to Al Schreiber. He took a job as an investigator for the public defender's office, and began to make amends. Howard made telephone calls and chased down files and interviewed inmates. Howard did whatever he could to help all the eager young lawyers who wanted to be gladiators.

It was March, 1988 when the Florida Supreme Court finally suspended him. Howard heard it from a newspaper reporter, and the news was good. Howard was helped by all the good reports from doctors and laboratories, and all the good words from all those good people. Howard helped himself, with his new humility and his hard work, and his surrender.

He was suspended for just one year.

Howard knew that he would be a lawyer again, and he knew when and where. He went to the public defender's office, to Al Schreiber, and told him: "I want to stay here, for as long as you will have me."

The verdict

Howard sat on a hard, dark-wood bench outside the grand jury room, waiting for the most important verdict of his career. The narrow courthouse hallway smelled like a school, like whatever it is that janitors spread on schoolhouse floors. The door to the courtroom was closed, and Howard was outside.

No one goes into the grand jury room except the grand jury, the judge, the witnesses and the prosecutor. There is no defense lawyer in the grand jury room because there is no defendant. That is what the law says, but Howard knows better. Howard sat on that hard, dark-wood bench while the grand jury decided whether to indict Eddie Williams for first-degree murder.

Howard was a lawyer again, an assistant public defender again, and this was his first murder case since he came back. This was his first murder case since he stopped smoking cocaine. Howard did not think about smoking cocaine but he thought about smoking a cigarette. It would have to wait. Howard could not smoke in the hall outside the grand jury room and he could not leave the bench until the jury was done, until he could see, on paper, what he already knew.

Eddie was not guilty. Howard knew it because he already proved it. Eddie was arrested and locked up, and he lost his business. The police said he did it and the prosecutor said he did it, and that was enough to get Eddie's picture on the television. Eddie didn't mind so much for himself as for his mother and his wife and his baby. It wasn't Eddie's first time in jail.

Eddie was 23 years old and he could not remember a time when he wasn't in trouble. He quit high school to mow lawns, but there were people who said Eddie really made his living by selling drugs and stealing. Some of those people were cops, and they visited Eddie often, whenever he fit the description of a suspect.

Eddie fit a lot of descriptions.

He was big: six-foot-two and 210 pounds. And he was black, but not very dark. He had a square head and a square face that was not quite big enough for all of its parts. All of the parts of Eddie's face were too big, and none looked like they belonged to the same man as any of the others. He had big, comic-book cheeks and a short, wrinkled forehead, like a wrinkled dog, with a short, thick scar that looked like a worm, right in the center. His teeth were capped in gold, all of them, and he had two words tattooed on his right forearm: PUBLIC ENEMY. The letters were crooked, as though they were drawn by a child. Eddie tattooed his own arm with a knife and ink, in jail.

Eddie spent nine months in jail on two charges of attempted murder, even though he insisted he was innocent, even though there were no witnesses. Police said Eddie made the witnesses disappear. They said he agreed to meet two men in a park for a drug deal, but he shot them and took the drugs and the money. The men were found alive. They said Eddie did it, but when they recovered, they vanished before they could testify. Eddie stayed in jail from December 1987 to September 1988, waiting for a trial that never began. He got out when he finally pleaded guilty to aggravated battery and was put on probation. The police were not pleased with Eddie, and they went back to visit him, often.

After that, Eddie would not have to commit a crime to go to jail. He could be locked up any time if he violated his probation—if he hung around with criminals or carried a gun or missed an appointment with his probation officer. But for more than a year, no one saw Eddie do anything except mow lawns and go home after work. No one even suspected Eddie until two days after Randy Kidd was murdered.

Even in South Florida, where everyday murder stopped being news a long time ago, Randy Kidd's murder was front-page stuff. Randy was a good man from a good family. His parents were teachers, and he was a high school football star who grew up and moved away but never forgot his friends and never stopped making new ones. He would walk up to people and shake hands with his powerful grip and say: "Hi, I'm Randy Kidd. How do you like me so far?"

He wore funny hats. He made one out of tongue depressors, and he had another one with lobster claws on top. He was an artist who sold art supplies and lived in Orlando, but he often drove 200 miles to his parents' home near Fort Lauderdale, just to see them and to bring presents he made. He brought a stained glass angel and a jewelry box. He had a special reason for the trip on Friday, Feb. 2, 1990, and a special present to deliver. He was coming home for his father's 78th birthday. Weeks before, his mother helped him sneak away with Rex Kidd's 1951 master's diploma from the University of Florida, and Randy had it framed. He laid it on the passenger seat of his yellow 1974 Porsche 914. It was just after 8 p.m., after dark, when he pulled into the parking lot of the C&S Bank about three miles from his parents' house.

Randy stood in line at the automatic teller with all the people who wanted money for the weekend. When it was his turn, he took out $120. He turned to the woman behind him and smiled. "It's all yours," he said, and walked to his car. The woman put her card in the machine and she heard a car start and then she heard another noise. Then she heard Randy Kidd shout: "I'm shot, I'm shot." She turned and saw him lying next to his car, bleeding, and she saw a man holding a gun. He was a tall, heavy black man wearing a green, pinstriped, knitted shirt. The killer ran, the police came and Randy died without saying another word. His money was gone.

Two nights later, the police went to visit Eddie Williams again. Someone told them that Eddie was the killer, that Eddie was even bragging about it. The police went to Eddie's house, but Eddie wasn't home. He hadn't been home for days, his wife said. The police went looking for Eddie, but he was gone. When he called home the next day, Eddie's wife told him the police wanted him. Eddie sounded surprised. "I'll come home tomorrow," he said, and he did, just before 6 o'clock in the evening. The police were waiting. "Where have you been," they asked, but Eddie wouldn't say. They took Eddie to jail, and they took Eddie's picture.

The police put it in a pile of other pictures of other black men and they called the woman who stood in line with Randy Kidd at the bank. She came to the police station and looked at the pictures and she picked out the only man wearing a green and white shirt. It was Eddie Williams. He was booked on a charge of first-degree murder 2:18 a.m.

They shuffled Eddie back down the long hallway about six hours later, hands cuffed behind, through the tunnel that crosses the street from the jail to the courthouse. The television cameras were waiting. Eddie James "Cortez" Williams told the judge he was innocent, and then they took him back to his cell. The guards brought him out one more time that day, to the interview room, so he could meet Howard Finkelstein, his lawyer.

Eddie had never heard of Howard. In Eddie's time, there was no ponytailed gladiator fighting for poor people, and he wouldn't know about a rich, white lawyer who drove an Eldorado and smoked cocaine and got locked up in that same jail. Eddie had his own problems. When Eddie said, again, that he was innocent, he did not expect this little man with the long hair to believe him. But Howard did believe him. Even Howard didn't expect that.

Howard read the police report before going to the jail and thought it was an awful case to begin his comeback. The client fit the description, the witness picked him out, another witness heard him confess. Howard was ready to go through the motions, work for a plea bargain and try to keep this poor man out of the electric chair, but he did not expect to believe.

Then he met Eddie. When he sat across from him, and listened to him, when Eddie became a real human being in his eyes and mind, Howard felt ashamed and he wondered: "Who am I to decide that this man is guilty? Who am I to want everything to be so easy?"

Howard looked at Eddie, and he listened. It was easier to be blind, to believe, as Howard once did, that everyone is innocent, or that everyone is guilty. Now that Howard had his soul back, and his spirit, and his sight, he had to use them and trust them. He listened to Eddie, and his instincts told him Eddie was not the killer.

They talked for a long time, about Eddie's life and Eddie's family, about mowing lawns, about getting arrested. Eddie told Howard where he was when Randy Kidd was shot. Eddie was out of town with his girlfriend, but he wanted Howard to know that he still loved his wife. Howard believed that, too. Listening to Eddie is like listening to a child, Howard thought. Eddie talked like a child, in a slow, high, soft voice. Eddie talked like a frightened child.

"I'm scared," he said. "I'm scared I'm going to get death. If this lady saw me in the pictures, how come she didn't see my teeth or my scar? How could she think some other guy looks like me?"

Eddie talked slow, but he did not hesitate the way a man does when he is measuring his words, the way a man does when he is lying. Eddie just talked, and Howard believed him.

Howard looked at Eddie and thought: "I believe him, but a jury won't." Howard looked at Eddie's teeth and Eddie's scar and Eddie's tattoo and he thought: "Eddie is every white juror's nightmare." Howard did not think he could put on any show that would compete with Eddie's face. As much as he loved the courtroom, Howard could not let this case go that far. Howard told Eddie not to worry and Howard went back to his office and worried.

The prosecution had a witness who identified Eddie and another witness who claimed he heard Eddie confess. That was enough for an indictment. That was probably enough for a conviction in a place where so many jurors were old white men and old white women who moved to Florida to get away from people who looked like Eddie. Howard thought an investigator could find Eddie's girlfriend, and one of them did, but she was no more credible than Eddie. Howard had to prove the witnesses were wrong.

Prove? Howard never proved. Howard made people doubt, just as he made himself doubt, and it nearly killed him. The new Howard, this new lawyer, had to be different. Howard promised the judge that if he got the chance, he would work harder than ever, and now it was time. Howard got out his law books for the first time in years and searched for a way to free Eddie Williams.

He already knew what the prosecutor was going to do next. He was going to make Eddie stand in a live lineup, because a live lineup is more believable than photos. Howard was certain that if it happened, Eddie would be the only one wearing a green-striped shirt, and after that, Eddie would be on his way to the electric chair.

Howard sat in his office, with his books, and every once in a while he looked up at the walls, for inspiration. Howard's new office was decorated just like Howard's first office, just like Howard's dorm room in college, except that there were no piles of clothes and records on the floor. Howard covered the walls with pictures of the people who inspired him: Jimi Hendrix, setting his guitar on fire; the Beatles, after Sgt. Pepper; an Al Pacino poster from the movie And Justice For All; Alcee Hastings, his old friend who was now a federal judge and who was about to be impeached; and Ronald Reagan. Reagan did not normally inspire Howard, but this picture did. It was a picture of Howard shooting the bird at a life-size cardboard cutout of the former president.

Howard looked at the walls and he looked in his books and he waited for inspiration. He was nearly exhausted when he found it: a Supreme Court ruling that said the state could not force anyone to stand in a lineup without a lawyer.

Howard grasped this, and it felt like the good, heavy lever he needed to pry Eddie loose. When the prosecutor asked for a lineup, Howard asked for a hearing. The judge agreed to listen, but not for long. He started by asking Howard a question. The judge asked Howard: "What are we doing here?"

Howard smiled.

"Your honor," he said, "we are going to figure that out together."

The ruling Howard found did not say a lawyer could stop a lineup, or change a lineup. It said only that he could be there. The prosecutor said he didn't mind having Howard at the lineup, and he wanted to go ahead right away.

"But if I have a right to be there," Howard said, "I must have a purpose, and if you are here listening to me, you must have a purpose. We must all have a role to play in this lineup, and in this case."

The judge agreed to listen a while longer, and Howard proceeded to think out loud about what their roles might be. Howard talked for hours, and then he offered an idea: Eddie would stand in a lineup if Howard could help pick the others, to be sure it was fair.

The prosecutor said he never heard of such a thing, but he had heard of Howard. After Howard was arrested, he wrote a letter to a judge that helped keep Howard out of jail. He was willing to go along.

Eddie stood in a lineup, but this time, the woman who stood behind Randy Kidd did not pick Eddie Williams. She was certain, in fact, that he wasn't the man at all. The killer was much younger.

Howard did not gloat. He sat down with the prosecutor and the detective and told them he knew they wanted the truth as much as he did. He asked them to reopen the investigation, and they agreed. Two weeks later, they told Howard they found the real killer. He was a 15-year old high school student.

Howard could have left it at that, but he sat on the hard, dark bench outside the grand jury room, waiting. When the prosecutor came out, he walked straight to Howard and handed him a single sheet of paper with the jury's decision: "Eddie James Williams a/k/a/ "Cortez" on the 2nd day of February unlawfully and feloniously and from a premeditated design to effect the death of a human being, namely Randy Kidd, did kill and murder the said Randy Kidd by shooting him with a firearm, to-wit, a handgun."

Across the typed page, in letters that looked like the tattoo letters on Eddie's forearm, the foreman of the grand jury wrote: "No True Bill." Eddie was officially cleared. The prosecutor shook Howard's hand. After that, a lot of people shook Howard's hand.

"Congratulations," he heard. "You are back, and you saved a man no one else cared about. You are the ponytailed gladiator again." But Howard didn't think so, and he didn't say so.

Howard didn't say any of the things people expected. When the reporters asked how he did this remarkable thing, Howard said he was lucky, and so was Eddie. Howard said the judge was fair and good, and the prosecutor was fair and good and the police were fair and good, but he was just lucky. Howard knew he was, in many ways.

Exactly one week before the grand jury cleared Eddie, Harry Gulkin asked a judge to clear Howard. Harry argued that Howard should be released early from probation because his record was exemplary. He passed all his drug tests, and he donated far more time than ordered talking about drug addiction at schools and drug centers and prisons. He really was working hard, and honorably, and standing up as a father and husband.

The judge agreed. Two years and eight months after he crashed into the police car, Howard was not guilty and Howard was free. Every night that Eddie lay in that cell, thinking about death, Howard lay in his bed, feeling his belly. Howard lay next to Donna, and listened for his daughters.

Saria was almost three years old, and Shayna was nearly six months. One or the other or both would cry and wake him up, every night, and Howard thought that was wonderful. Howard could lie in his own bed, listening for his daughters, poking at his belly, without worrying about men with shotguns, or about electricity shooting from the walls, or about going to prison, or about losing his license, or about dying.

Now Howard knew: What next? Another day in a good life,

a far better life than he had any right to expect or to complain about. Howard did not worry about anything, except his belly fat, and except this: Howard worried that he would never be the ponytailed gladiator again.

He knew he could be a lawyer, in an office, reading books, but that was different. Howard wasn't sure he could be the lawyer who lent his vision to juries, who made them see what he saw, and made them believe. How did he ever make them see when he was so blind?

Howard wondered, and he did not find out the answer until he met Octavious Williams.

A gladiator once more

Octavious Williams killed a man he met in a bar.

He was not supposed to be in that bar, or any bar, because he was 17 years old and he was out of prison on parole. He was supposed to be at home, in bed, but he was out in bars in the middle of the night.

He shot a stranger and he did not seem at all sorry. Howard wasn't sure he could help a young man so angry, but he felt obligated to try. Octavious and Eddie Williams shared more than the coincidence of last name.

They were young and black and mowed lawns, when they worked, and they lived on the west side of Fort Lauderdale. Black people had lived there since they came to help build the city. They tacked up tarpaper shacks where they wouldn't be in the white folks' way, and the years had not brought them closer.

Howard, the good hippie, the good liberal, was no more blind to their black skin than anyone else and he did not try to be.

Howard saw so many young, black men in trouble, so many more than when he began working as a public defender. He did not believe they were all innocent, but he was more frightened than ever of people who believed they were all guilty. Howard had been judged, and Howard been treated kindly, but he could not say that judgment was fair.

How was it fair that a white lawyer, who knew better, should be set free after he crashed into a police car, blind on cocaine? How was that fair when so many young, black men went to jail every day and stayed in jail, with no bail-bond pals or drug counselors to rescue them? Howard knew that he hadn't killed anyone, but he might have, and he hadn't stolen anything, but he never had to. Howard never had to rob a store to pay for his drugs. Nobody gave these young, black men shoeboxes filled with cash, unless they sold cocaine.

When Howard stood up to be judged, he did not stand alone. He had a roomful of judges and lawyers and doctors to plead for him. When these young, black men stood up to be judged, they stood by themselves, with gold teeth and tattoos and ragged scars. Howard believed, more than ever, that it was his place to stand by their side, but he was less sure then ever that he could help.

Octavious had none of Eddie's grotesque features, but his anger and his color could still frighten a white jury into punishing him. He was not big, just five-foot-seven and 150 pounds, but he was all sinew and muscle and all to a purpose. Even sitting still, thick muscles lifted his young, smooth skin and stretched it tight across his veins.

The upper muscle of his left arm swelled with a tattoo that advertised his anger: TNT. Octavious did not draw it himself.

He was born in Newark, N.J., but his mother sent him to live with her parents in Florida when he was very young. Octavious never met his father. Octavious did not know his father's name. His academic record ended in the tenth grade, but his criminal record kept growing: aggravated battery, armed robbery, burglary. He had exhausted the state's patience and resources for juvenile offenders. Octavious graduated from youth homes to county jail to state prison. This new charge could send him back for the rest of his life.

The night Octavious became a killer, he went to a bar to drink and to meet people. He met a man named Garfield Farquharson, and a few hours later, he killed him. Octavious ran straight home after that, and he was still there the next day when he was arrested. The police told him he did not have to let them in without talking to a lawyer first, but he let them in anyway and he talked. Octavious wanted them to know one thing: he was not afraid.

He told Howard the same thing when they finally met, a day later. "I'm not afraid of the cops and I'm not afraid of the judge and I'm not afraid of you," he said. "And it wouldn't matter if I was. No white judge'll give me a break."

Howard looked into his client's eyes and knew he was lying about not being afraid. Howard was not afraid anymore, not the way he was when he looked into Benjamin LeParre's eyes, but he knew fear well enough to recognize it. Howard looked into Octavious' eyes and wondered: Where does a kid that age learn this? Where does he learn to spit at people who are trying to help him? Howard knew that he had to be a teacher before he could be a lawyer, and he had to teach quickly.

"Octavious," he said, "if you are not afraid, you are stupid, and I don't think you are stupid. You've gotten plenty of breaks, and you know it. That's why you were on probation, but you didn't know a good break when you got one. So cut the bullshit. If you listen to me, and if we are both real, real lucky, you might not spend the rest of your life in a real prison, with killers. If you act tough with me and the judge and the jury, you'll wind up being somebody's wife."

Octavious did not give in at once, but he did give in. Each time Howard came to talk, Octavious glared a little less and snorted a little less and flexed his tattoo a little less. In the months after his arrest, as his trial approached, Octavious was learning to act like what he was: 17, and scared.

Howard was sure that would help. He was not sure it would help enough. No matter who told the story of the night Garfield Farquharson died, it always ended the same: Octavious killed him, and then he ran away. Howard had to find a way for a jury to make sense of that without coming to the obvious conclusion.

When Howard was a young lawyer learning how much a courtroom really was like television, he also learned an important difference. He learned that there aren't really two sides to a story, or three or five or eight. There aren't sides at all. Stories come in pieces, dozens of them, hundreds of them. Every witness throws pieces into the pile and it doesn't really matter where they came from. Some lawyers are good at picking out the right pieces and holding them up to a jury. Some aren't. Howard was very good, and Octavious was very lucky. There were a lot of ugly pieces in the pile even before his trial began.

All agreed that Farquharson went out that Monday night, Nov. 19, 1989, looking for fun. He was wearing Nike high-tops with white socks, blue-jean pants with a red, yellow and green belt, and a short-sleeve denim jacket over a black tank top. He had a gold bracelet on his right wrist and three gold rings.

Farquharson was no criminal, but he was a drug addict. He used to smoke cocaine. He went into treatment a year before, and he was clean for a long time, but lately he was drinking. His blood was full of alcohol the night he died, nearly twice the legal limit, but he was so used to it that even the police didn't notice until it was too late.

He liked to go to bars and have a good time, and let everyone know he could afford it. At 26, he owned a construction company with his brother and father, and he told people he made a lot of money. He was proud of his maroon 1988 BMW 528E and he was not shy about mentioning the price: $35,000. He drove it that night to the Domino Club, where he was sure to find other Jamaicans who wanted to have a good time. There was one parking space left, and one other car heading in that direction.

Farquharson and the other driver got out and argued, but the argument didn't last long. The other driver had a gun. Some of the people in the parking lot said Farquharson had one too. There were shots, but no one was hit. Farquharson drove away, but he had left the first pieces Howard needed.

The people who saw Farquharson at the next bar that night said he was angry, so angry he was talking to himself. He kept asking: "Does anybody have a gun?"

"Maybe Tay has one," someone said. That is when Garfield Farquharson met Octavious Williams, who liked to be called by his second-syllable nickname. They left the bar together, but they weren't alone.

From there on, the pieces scattered. There were pieces that showed Octavious getting a gun from home, or from a friend. There were pieces that showed Farquharson offering him money, then taking it back because the gun didn't work. There were pieces that showed Octavious trying to shoot the gun to prove it did. There was a piece that showed Octavious keeping the gun, and a piece that showed Farquharson keeping the gun.

All the pieces showed them getting into the BMW and driving away together, and having more drinks.

The Fort Lauderdale police stopped the car sometime after 3:30 in the morning. An officer spotted the license plate that was broadcast after the shooting at the Domino Club. He said Farquharson was pleasant and cooperative, and so were the man and woman in the back seat. He did not think Farquharson was drunk. There was also a quiet young man who stood off by himself and said nothing. The police frisked the men, but they didn't find a gun. They let everyone go.

After that, there were more scattered pieces: Farquharson still talking about revenge, Octavious saying he wanted to go home, Farquharson calling him a baby and saying he would spank him. The car stopped just before 4 a.m., at 2925 NW 10th Court. Octavious got out, then Farquharson got out. They were shouting at each other.

The medical examiner provided the last piece, the one that connected the shouting to Octavious running away: Farquharson was shot directly between the eyes, point-blank.

Howard picked carefully at the pieces, but he was not satisfied, because he could not make them fit the way Octavious needed. Octavious told him they struggled, that Farquharson punched him and was going to punch him again. Farquharson was four inches taller, eight or 10 pounds heavier, and Octavious was losing the fight until he saw the gun sticking out from Farquharson's belt. He grabbed it and swung it hard against the taller man's face. The gun fired by itself, he said. The gun that hadn't fired all night suddenly went off by itself.

Howard picked at the pieces, but he could not make them fit. If Octavious hit Farquharson across the face with a heavy gun, why was there no bruise? Why was there only a gunshot wound, right between the eyes?

He kept looking for the piece to answer it, but he knew even before that trial that Octavious would not be the last man to attack Garfield Farquharson. Howard would have to do it himself. Howard believed it must have taken more than a construction job, even as a partner, to buy that BMW. Howard believed that a man who bought cocaine might sell cocaine, and a man who did either might frighten someone into killing him.

There was a time when Howard might have picked up those pieces and hurled them at a dead man without a second thought, but he thought about himself and then he thought about the dead man's family. Before the trial began, Howard walked up to Garfield Farquharson's family in the courthouse hallway and introduced himself.

"I am going to say certain things about drug addiction and what it can do to a man," Howard said. "I want you to know I am not saying these things to be mean. I want you to know that I understand, because I am a drug addict."

Howard kept picking through the pieces as the trial began, but he wanted the jury to make the first choice. He wanted the jury to choose him. Howard wanted the jury to focus its attention on the ponytailed gladiator, not on the black teenager.

Howard wore a dark-blue, pinstriped suit, straight off the boys' rack, that lit up his sandy, glistening hair. Howard had talked the swagger out of his client and into himself. Howard swaggered up to the front of the courtroom and stood there, on the balls of his feet, bouncing just a little, like a diver getting ready to leap. He was smiling from the moment he walked into court, and it was the soft, casual smile of confidence, not the hard, ruler-edged smile of a man trying too hard. That is how good an actor Howard could be in a courtroom. His smile was a lie, but it was impossible to tell.

His smile was a lie because there was no joy in coming back, not to this case, not yet. The day Octavious Williams went on trial in room 910 of the Broward County Courthouse — March 15, 1990 — Howard went on trial, too. This would be the first jury he faced since he got his license back, two weeks to the day after a judge set Howard free from the rest of his probation term because of his exemplary record in recovery.

Howard knew that he could make juries believe or doubt, and he could make judges throw out laws and he could set men free when no one else believed he could.

Now he would find out if he could do it sober.

He began to believe he could when he looked at the jurors and saw them looking at him. "Keep looking," Howard said to himself. "Keep looking at me."

Howard could not hide Octavious, but he did hide the tattoo under a long-sleeved, pressed shirt. "Look at Octavious," he said, and he put his left hand on his client's right shoulder. Octavious stood up, smiled and nodded politely, and then he sat down—all just as Howard told him to do. Howard gave the jury one look and took their eyes back.

"Look at my hair," Howard said, as though anyone had missed it. That is when he asked them not to hold it against his client, and when he knew he won them over.

If there was anyone in the court who could take attention away from Howard, it was the prosecutor, but that was not good for him. He was six feet, eight inches tall. He was as tall sitting in his chair as Howard was standing up. Howard could not believe his luck. Nobody roots for the bigger man.

The jury was barely seated when Howard could feel the answer inside himself: He could do this. All those years, he believed the drugs helped him see, but now he knew the truth, and Donna was right. He had pushed through the black curtain, and he could see everything. Howard could see and he could hear. For the next week, Howard could hear the questions coming from his mouth as though he were hearing them for the first time, as though he had never had to think about them at all, as though he were meant to say them.

Howard put the pieces together this way: Farquharson had the gun all along. He couldn't find the men who shot at him so he took his anger out on this boy who only wanted to go home. Octavious was only trying to defend himself, and he ran because he was so scared when that gun went off.

The prosecutor fit the puzzle differently: Octavious had the gun all night, although he hid it from the cops when they searched the car. He was angry that Farquharson wouldn't buy it from him, and angrier still at Farquharson's insults. When Farquharson finally threw him out of the car, Octavious simply called him out and blew his head open.

The jury might have believed either, except for the final piece.

"I was wrong," the medical examiner said. "This man was not shot between the eyes. He was shot below the nose. I was wrong because his face was so badly broken, as though someone smashed it with the gun and the gun suddenly went off on the way down."

That was all Howard needed, and all Octavious needed. Howard soared through his closing argument, pointing a finger to the prosecutor.

"He wants you to find Octavious guilty," Howard told the jurors. "But I ask you — no, I implore you..."

Howard ran from juror to juror, asking each, by name, to please let Octavious go free. They did, but Howard didn't. Before Octavious could walk away, Howard took him by the arm and sat him down in a back room and asked him this question: "Now do you understand that you got a break?"

Howard didn't wait for answer.

"Just don't forgot what I told you, and don't forget that if this happens again, I won't be there to help you," he said. "If this happens again, you go down for good. Go back north, with your mother, to a different place and get away from these people and all this trouble. Go away."

And then he told Octavious this: "Get away from drugs."

Making sense in the '90s

The last car Eddie Williams drove was a Cadillac.

The man Howard saved from the electric chair was parked behind a bar when two men with submachine guns walked up and fired into a 1983 Coupe de Ville. They killed Eddie, and they killed a 16-year-old boy who was standing next to the car talking to him.

It was 10 p.m. July 14, 1990, a little over four months since Howard freed Eddie from jail. The last time Howard saw him, Eddie came to Howard's office with a thank-you gift that Howard could not accept: a gold bracelet inscribed Number One Lawyer. Eddie told Howard he wanted to sue the police for false arrest, and Howard gave him the name of a friend who handled that sort of case. Eddie called and made an appointment, but he didn't live long enough to keep it.

The shooting was spectacular enough to get Eddie's picture in all the papers one last time. The stories all mentioned Howard, and they all made him sick.

Was there any sense to this? Howard saved Eddie from a murder charge so that Eddie could die in a drug deal. If Howard hadn't saved him, would Eddie be alive, or would he have died another way? It wasn't just Eddie's death that made Howard feel sick. It was that he couldn't know. "Is it all random? All of it? If it is, what am I doing?"

Howard hated himself for thinking this, but he did: At least Eddie wasn't the killer. If Eddie dragged that poor boy into it, that was awful, but at least Eddie didn't pull the trigger. At least Eddie wasn't Robert Sherwood.

Life as the ponytailed gladiator was more fun when the stakes were largely philosophical. Nobody died sleeping on the beach or watching dirty videos or cursing at cops. Life was more fun then, but it was more important now that Howard was a father and a husband and the chief assistant public defender for Broward County.

Howard's good work won him a promotion, and Howard finally came to believe he deserved the job, if not the money. He decided that he did not deserve $70,000 a year, but his children did. So he took it. Once in a while, he wondered how much money he made and lost in private practice, how much money he smoked or gave away, but he could not figure it out. Once he guessed $1 million, and he laughed. Could it really be? It could, but it didn't matter. Howard would not waste this good time worrying about money.

Howard had too much else to think about. He had to think about Eddie and Andy and all the others, and whether life and death were random events. Whether there really was a transcendent truth. He did not think about Roger. Four years after the crash, it was still too hard to think about the man who stole his soul, and Howard did not know that Roger finally went to prison. The police arrested Roger a half-dozen times for his cocaine and his guns, and once when he shot up his girlfriend's apartment house with an automatic rifle. Howard did not know that Roger went to prison the very day he crashed into the police car.

Howard set aside time every day to meditate, and he still does. After he stretches and lifts runs through his neighborhood, Howard closes his eyes and clears his mind and lets his thoughts find their natural order. Every day, Saria and Shayna and Donna rise to the top. Every day, he understands a little more about the others.

Free of fear, free of drugs, Howard could feel a good and greater force filling his mind and pulling him along. He is certain, now, that there is a path, and he has found it, but he is still not certain whether he has choice. Howard found his God, not the fearsome God of scripture poised to prod or punish, but a spirit that bound him to his family and to this earth and to other men. Howard believes his God has a plan, because he could not believe that all of it just happened for no reason.

Howard thought about Eddie and about Andy and the others who fell and died, and Howard thought about himself, and how he fell but lived. It didn't make sense without a reason. Howard decided the reason was his work. Howard believes his God was testing him, but He saved Howard so that Howard could save Eddie and Octavious and others to come, and it is not up to Howard to judge them or keep them or follow them the rest of their lives.

Howard believes, but Howard does not believe blindly, because he knows what that can lead to, and he cannot forgive himself. Howard is still too angry for that. He is still looking for a way to understand why he could not have fallen without being so mean, so petty, so weak.

So Howard feels his belly and he meditates. Howard thinks about what he believes, and every day, he believes a little more, even though it is easier just to believe and not think at all.

Howard prays that he will always believe, because it would be too hard to go back, to be tested again. The last test was the most frightening of all.

He had been free nearly four years when he woke up one morning and grabbed his head. Howard felt as though someone had pushed a sword through his ears. He lay still and hoped the pain would go away, but it didn't, and his eyes began to twitch. Howard went to the doctor.

"It is nothing serious," the doctor said. "It is just an infection, but it will be painful until the antibiotics work." He asked Howard: "Have you ever taken Percodan?"

Howard filled the prescription on the way home, and he did not tell Donna. Howard went straight to his room and took his antibiotics and his Percodan and he felt much better, very soon. "There is nothing wrong with this," Howard told himself. "I will take the Percodan only for pain," he said, and soon he took another, and another one after that. When Howard woke up the next day, he did not remember the terrible pain in his head. All he could remember was the Percodan, and he went straight for it, and he began to shake.

Howard suddenly shook free of himself and stepped back to watch the sweating man fumble with the bottle top. Howard saw the sweating man, and he felt his heart pounding and his breath running short. "I remember that man," Howard said. "He is a drug addict." Howard picked up the bottle and ran downstairs and threw it in the garbage.

Howard had wondered about this day for four years, but it was not what he imagined. Howard heard what the doctors said and what the counselors said and what he said to other people, but he always wanted to believe he was different. Howard wanted to believe there would be a time when he could have one glass of wine with dinner or a drink with friends, or when he could come home from the office and light a joint. Now he knew he never would.

He told Donna, and she cursed him and hugged him, all at once. "You are only human," she told Howard. "Do you know that now?"

Howard felt sure he did. He pulled on his running shorts, walked out onto the patio and poked his belly. He decided to run at least an extra mile.

Only human

Howard finally came to believe he was only human, but Cynthia Thomas did not believe it and she never would.

At first, and for a long time, she didn't believe anything Howard said—not about the law, not about cocaine, not about life or death. She just glared and wondered what this little white man in a suit wanted from her.

She knew this: All men wanted something, and it was never anything good.

The best man she had ever known was her father, and he was drunk even when he was home. Cynthia's mother did her best to love and feed six children and warn them about the dangers of the world, but Cynthia did not feel loved and she did not listen to her mother. When she graduated from Fort Lauderdale High School, Cynthia Thomas decided she knew enough and moved away from home.

She went to Washington, D.C. and got a job at a K-Mart. She worked hard enough to be promoted, twice, and made more money than she ever dreamed she would. One day, Cynthia walked into a car dealership and bought a brand-new Mazda GLC, right off the showroom floor. It was the proudest day of her life. If she had listened to her mother, there would have been many more.

Instead, Cynthia listened to any man who promised to love her. She listened to men who gave her cocaine and showed her how to shoot it into her arms and smoke it out of pipes. She listened to men who told her how she could make more money than any cashier at K-Mart. Cynthia listened to men instead of listening to her mother, and she lost her job and her new car and her dignity.

When she finally moved back home more than a dozen years after leaving with her diploma, she was a drug addict and she was dying.

Cynthia figured that out before any doctor told her. She had seen her friends grow weak and die, and she heard people whisper as she walked past. She heard them say she had the look of death on her face. For years after she first heard that, Cynthia would not look in a mirror. She could not face her death any more than she could face her life, which was getting worse by the day.

The first time Cynthia was arrested, for possession of cocaine, she was ashamed. The second time, for selling cocaine, she was just angry. The judge put her on probation, but she could not stay away from drugs and she went to state prison for 15 months. When she got out, she went right back to smoking crack and she was arrested again and again. Each time, she got angrier.

Finally, the doctors told her what she suspected all along: She was dying of AIDS. Instead of jail, they sent her to a hospice. She ran away.

The next time Cynthia was arrested, six months later, she told police something shocking. She said she'd had sex with 100 men because she wanted them all to die.

She was not prepared for the reaction. Cynthia Thomas, who could not keep a job as a K-Mart cashier, became an instant celebrity as the AIDS Hooker of Death.

All the other times Cynthia had been arrested, no one cared. This time, there were television cameras and reporters and everyone in the crowded courtroom was staring. Cynthia felt lonelier and angrier and more afraid than ever. When the judge asked if she had a lawyer, she just stared straight ahead and shook her head. She was startled to hear a strange voice answer for her.

"Yes she does your honor," Howard Finkelstein said. "I'm her lawyer."

Howard will always remember that moment, because it was as important to him as it was to Cynthia. It was the moment Howard stopped wondering why he was alive.

No one on this earth sent him to Cynthia. No one assigned him her case or wrote her name on his calendar or circled her hearing on the court docket. When Howard heard what the television reporters were saying about her, he knew it was his place to help.

That is why Cynthia did not believe he was human.

"He is an angel," she says. "He is an angel sent from God."

Howard bows his head when he hears this and the harder he shakes it to disagree, the harder she nods to insist it is so. Cynthia is sitting next to Howard in the bright morning light shining through the front window of Broward House. Everyone who lives there has AIDS.

Howard helped find Cynthia a place there. Now, months after coming to her rescue in court, he has come to her side again. He has been visiting at least once a week to talk to Cynthia, hold her hand and remind himself how lucky he is.

There is an odd sort of cheeriness about this place where everyone is dying. Howard and Cynthia sit in the big room at one of the long, Colonial-style dining tables. Behind them, along the front wall of the building, are high windows that let in plenty of sun to burn away the antiseptic smell.

Beyond the tables there are couches and recliners and a new, big-screen television. The television is on but no one is sitting in front of it. Everyone is on the move, chatting in groups, walking in and out the front door, circling the room. One woman begins singing, loud and strong, to the sound of a commercial for a diet program.

"Come on and Nutrasize your body!" she sings, and then she laughs very hard. She does not have to worry about dieting.

Several people call to Howard. Some know him from his visits. Others know him from the newspapers. And others know him as their lawyer and friend.

Everyone is dressed casually, in jeans or shorts, except Howard and Cynthia. Howard is wearing a blue lawyer suit.

Cynthia is wearing a trim, tan cotton blouse and skirt with black stockings.

Her makeup is a little thick, but she is just learning to wear it, for the first time in her life, now that she can look in a mirror again. She is resting her thin, right hand on Howard's left shoulder and she is crying, on and off.

"When I met him, I didn't believe him," she says. "I was so scared, I didn't believe anybody. I thought he was like all the others."

But Howard did not just leave her after court, like the other lawyers. Just as Harry did for him nearly five years before, Howard persuaded a judge to give Cynthia another chance. Instead of sending her to jail, the judge offered her treatment for her addiction and her infection. Howard and Cynthia both know that another lawyer might have gotten her the same chance. But only Howard could have made her take it.

Howard told her what a second chance meant to him, and he kept coming back to hold her hand through treatment. When he couldn't come, he called or sent notes.

He sent one note that said only this: "Love yourself."

"No one ever said that to me before," Cynthia says. "Howard showed me how to be loved."

Howard hugs Cynthia and whispers a few private words before he steps outside, into the heat. It is an exceptionally bright day, even for South Florida. The sun glares off the greasy asphalt parking lot, off every white-tile rooftop, off every window and car hood and palm frond.

It is as bright as a northern winter day when the sun glares off the snow. Howard squints and blinks, but he can see just fine. There is something else Howard will never understand about Cynthia, but that he will always admire.

"I got sober to live," he says. "Cynthia got sober to die."

For all he learned in law school and in courtrooms, for all he learned in treatment centers and in jail, Howard learned his most important lessons from a 37-year-old black drug addict dying of AIDS.

"The notes I sent to Cynthia didn't take three seconds out

of my day," he says. "And the visits? It's time that I used to waste being angry. Now that I'm not so angry, I have more time to love."

Howard pauses a moment before continuing.

"I still want to be loved, too," he says. "But now I know you can't beat people into loving you. You have to earn it."

Two familiar voices

Donna answered the telephone. She did not know who this woman was, asking for her husband.

Howard knew the moment he heard her voice.

It had been a dozen years since she left him, and Kelly had been living in California, in the commune, all that time. Now she was back and she wanted to see him. Howard was not at all sure he liked the idea.

Every time he thought of Kelly, he felt ashamed.

Of all the people Howard loved and hurt, Kelly was the only one he offered no explanation or apology. She was the only one he'd been able to avoid, because she left.

All the rest, for whatever reasons, stayed with him or near him through the worst times. They were close enough to watch him go mad and suffer. Close enough to watch him come back again. Close enough to understand, if not forgive.

Kelly saw Howard turn selfish and mean, but she could not know how selfish or mean he became and she could not know why. Howard did not want to tell her. It was Donna who told him he should.

"Close this," she told him. "Close these open wounds, yours and hers, so you don't have to hide from any part of yourself."

Howard listened and decided she was right. He told Kelly he would meet her at the health club where she worked. All the way there, he thought about what he would say. And still, he was not sure what to expect. He never, ever expected to hear the voice behind him calling his name as he sat in the waiting room.

"Howard!"

Howard did not recognize this voice as quickly as Kelly's. He did not want to recognize it at all. It was deep but flat, with no trace of emotion. Howard could not tell if it was a friendly voice or an angry voice but he knew it was a voice he didn't want to hear.

Howard knew, before he turned around, that it was Roger's.

Howard did not hesitate to look straight at him. "There must be a reason for this," Howard thought. It would make no sense to waste time before finding out. But Roger spoke before Howard could.

"I read the story," he said.

Howard knew what that meant. Now that Howard was in the news again, for the right reasons, a local magazine ran a story about his best and worst times. The worst times were about Roger. Howard thought about the guns and bombs and shotgun blasts.

He hoped Roger would smile. He didn't.

"I wish I could say something about all that," Roger told him. "But I can't. I don't remember a whole lot. I remember some things. I remember a week or two at a time. But a lot of it just jumps around. I don't know what happened or what I dreamed. A lot of it's just missing."

Howard looked harder at Roger's face. He could not tell if the sneer was still there because Roger's face had turned doughy. The young, mean, tough guy was a jowly, middle-aged man trying to work off a few pounds at a health spa.

Howard believed what Roger said, because it sounded so familiar. Roger told Howard he'd been off drugs for five years. He got out of prison. He found a job. Roger showed no sign of remorse or joy or anger about any of it. He said he had to leave.

"I guess you'd like me to say I'm sorry," Roger said. "But I can't. I just don't remember enough."

In a moment, Roger was gone and Howard heard his name again.

Talking to Kelly was easier than he dared imagine. She was just as sweet, just as pretty, as he remembered. Howard started to tell her his story, and then he gave her a copy of the story from the magazine. She called him a few days later.

"I'm lucky," she said. "I'm lucky I'm not Donna. If I hadn't left when I did, it would have happened to me. I'm sure I'd be dead."

Howard and Kelly talked again after that, and again. Howard still does not remember much more than Roger did, but he did not let that stop him.

"I'm sorry," he said, and Kelly smiled. ☐

Redemption: An epilogue

October, 1999—The music, high and resonant, has Howard grinning and tapping the steering wheel.

"I love this song," he announces. "You've got to listen to this."

Twenty years ago, he'd have been talking about Janis Joplin wailing for her lost love. Today, it's Snoopy wailing for his late dinner.

Howard isn't driving a beat-up VW or a gussied-up Cadillac. He's driving a Chrysler minivan, the ultimate suburban mom-and-pop machine, with Donna in the passenger seat. It's the perfect vehicle for a couple whose lives revolve around their daughters: taking them to school, or to religious class at the Reconstructionist synagogue the family has joined.

Nothing you've read about Howard and Donna would help you pick them out of a crowd at a PTA social, and they're immensely proud of that. (Howard didn't cut off his ponytail, but he did prune it to near-vestigial modesty.)

"We're not the same people we were 10 years ago," Donna says. She pauses a moment. "We're not the same people we were five years ago." Donna finds it harder now to think about the early years of their marriage, much less talk about them. "I know that our experiences brought us to where we are, but I also know that we might have gotten here sooner, and better, without all that," she says. "I want my daughters to be strong, not to take drugs or stay in an abusive relationship."

Howard used to talk more about those times. He was a popular speaker at local schools for years, until everyone including Howard began to wonder if kids were getting the right message. "Some of them would look at me and think I was pretty cool," Howard says. "They'd say, "Cocaine didn't hurt you. You've done all right.' "

What those kids didn't know, and might not understand, is how much cocaine did hurt him, how lucky he was to survive—and how hard he's worked to become a different person.

The day I met Howard, he told me that the proof of his redemption would lie in what he could do for others. In the years since, the proof became both clear and abundant.

Throughout the 1990s, Howard championed the most vulnerable and often least-sympathetic clients whose cases were dumped on the public defender's office: The violent mentally ill. One of those clients did something so revolting that he was chased and beaten by an angry crowd: He knocked an old lady to the ground. She died the next day.

The state, Howard discovered, was not much different from the enraged crowd. His client, Aaron Wynn, had a history of arrests followed by beatings or neglect in institutions that were supposed to help him. Time after time, he was drugged into a stupor and left to lie in a heap. Time after time, his family had no idea where he'd been locked away—and no idea what to do when he was finally found and sent home.

Howard didn't just defend Wynn, he attacked the State of Florida. Howard demanded better care for all mentally ill defendants and he demanded the state obey the law that gives patients the right to a hearing before they can be drugged and locked away.

He won. Howard's crusade forced Florida to change the way it treats mentally ill defendants. His agitation helped lead to creation of the nation's first mental health court, a separate division to deal only with such cases.

A judge finally ordered the state to pay up to $18 million to get Aaron Wynn care for the rest of his life.

Howard became so closely identified with the cause of mental illness that a man threatening to leap from a rooftop in downtown Fort Lauderdale in March 1998 had only one request: He wanted to talk to Howard Finkelstein.

Howard talked him down and got him help. Getting help had become Howard's second career.

Once again a reliable source of quotes and quips, Howard was an obvious choice when a local television producer set out to find an expert commentator during the O.J. Simpson trial. Howard was asked to be a guest on Miami's WSVN news, one of the region's top-rated shows. Howard's appearance generated hundreds of calls and letters. He was asked back the next day, and the day after.

He wound up staying for the entire trial. Howard was such a hit that the station found a way to keep him long after the verdict. He became host of a regular consumer feature, "Help Me Howard," tackling complaints about leaky roofs and insurance rip-offs. Soon, others were offering to help Howard get a spot on a network program, or maybe a show of his own.

"That's not what I ever wanted," Howard says. "What I

Howard Finkelstein as OJ Simpson legal commentator at WSVN TV, Miami. Photograph *The Miami Herald,* September 28, 1995

have is perfect, an extension of what I've done in court. I can help people and still spend time with my family."

Whenever he's tempted, he says, he goes back and reads a story about a hippie lawyer who lost his way and about the terrible things that happened to him and the people he loved as a result.

He knows that he holds on to his life only as long as he holds on to his purpose.

Other ends

Ed Stack, the sheriff whose decency campaign gave Howard his first major public cause, died of complications from pneumonia in 1989. He was 79.

Harry Gulkin, the former judge who came to Howard's rescue after his arrest, died in 1991 of a heart attack. He was 50.

Channing Brackey, Howard's former partner, died of epilepsy in 1997. He was 48.

Cynthia Thomas, the client who suffered from AIDS, died in 1994.

Raymond "Little Ray" Thompson, Howard's biggest-name client, was convicted in 1986 of murder and of running a major drug-smuggling operation. He later pleaded guilty to two other murders. He is now appealing a sentence of death.

Barry "The Bear" Hunwick pleaded guilty to a single charge of murder in the case that made Howard fear for his life. It took 17 years. A police informant finally taped Hunwick confessing to the murder. Hunwick pleaded guilty in July 1999 and accepted a sentence of life in prison.

Octavious Williams, the teenager Howard defended after returning to the public defender's office, got married, had two children and became a deacon in his church.

About the author

Douglas Kalajian has been a journalist for more than 20 years. He is a former reporter and editor at the Miami Herald. He is now a feature writer at the Palm Beach Post. He lives in Boca Raton, Florida, with his wife, Robyn, and their daughter, Mandy.

Snow Blind is designed by Tom Suzuki, Tom Suzuki, Inc., Falls Church, Virginia. Cover design is also by Tom Suzuki.

The text is set 10.5 on 12.5 point Times Roman. The display typefaces are Futura bold and Emmascript

The book is printed by Lightning Print Inc., La Vergne, Tennessee.